Lessons from the Lives of the Saints

Lessons from the Lives of the Saints

Rev. Joseph M. Esper

Basilica Press
SAN DIEGO

Published by Basilica Press
Post Office Box 675205
Rancho Santa Fe, California 92067
www.basilica.com
(888) 396-2339

Cover design by Charlotte Johnson
99 00 01 02 03 15 14 13 12 11 10 09 08 07 06 05 04 03 02 01

Printed in the United States of America ∞
ISBN 1–930314–01–9

Basilica Press is a division of the Missionaries of Faith Foundation.

Contents

Introduction

Jesus sent His disciples out two by two (Mark 6:7), for He knew His followers would need to support one another in their proclamation of the Gospel and in their own efforts to live it out each day. This same reality exists here and now. Very few of us are called to a life of complete solitude; as a rule, we are meant to have the support and encouragement of the Christian community — especially in a world which increasingly denies God, opposes the Church, and rejects Gospel values. Along with the sacraments and our own personal prayer, we need — if we are to continue growing in wisdom and grace — regular interaction with others whose values and beliefs complement our own. This ongoing interaction and support need not be, and should not be, limited to those followers of Christ who are alive on earth now; after all, God's Kingdom is eternal, and all His followers are forever alive to Him (Luke 20:38). Thus, in addition to the angels, the Church offers us the saints as our spiritual friends, benefactors, and guides.

The holy men and women of every age who've gone before us and who now live with God in Heaven can, if we ask it of them, give us just as much inspiration and encouragement (and indeed, even more) as our fellow Christians whom we see in the flesh. We are spiritually surrounded by a great company of witnesses (Hebrews 12:1), all of whom desire our eternal happiness. In this regard, the saints are happy to intercede for us, pray for us, and serve as our role models; they are pleased when their own experiences on earth provide lessons, inspiration, and encouragement for those who come after them. Their prayers are very valuable, for Scripture tells us that the prayer of a holy person is powerful indeed (James 5:16); moreover, it pleases God when we admire and attempt to imitate those who've given themselves completely to Him.

Catholicism has always made a point of honoring and remembering its heroes — most especially the Virgin Mary, but many other persons as well. Such honor, of course, pales in comparison to the heavenly glory they experience for all eternity, but it nonetheless serves an important purpose: by honoring the saints, we glorify their Creator, and by remembering their teachings and example, we give ourselves excellent role models and guides for our own journey through life. For these reasons, the Church has incorporated the feast days of many different saints into its liturgical calendar, including apostles, martyrs, evangelists, missionaries, confessors, virgins, popes, bishops, priests, religious, and laypersons. Those canonized saints who do not have a particular feast day of their own are included in the Feast of All Saints [November 1], and in addition to honoring the vast, uncountable number of saints in Heaven (Revelation 7:9), the Church also remembers on the Feast of All Souls [November 2] our brothers and sisters still undergoing purification in Purgatory. This spiritual unity, or "communion of saints," aids the entire Church; according to the *Catechism of the Catholic Church*, "Exactly as Christian communion among our fellow pilgrims brings us closer to Christ, so our communion with the saints joins us to Christ, from Whom as its fountain and head issues all grace, and the life of the People of God itself" (no. 957).

This book is intended to make the wisdom and example of the saints more accessible and helpful to the average Catholic. A brief biography is given of each saint in the Church's liturgical year, along with several lessons or insights drawn from his or her life, presented in a manner which I hope will prove to be both practical and useful. The saints are not merely for us to admire and pray to; God also desires us to imitate them, for they — with the help of divine grace — successfully overcame many of the same troubles, worries, and temptations which beset us today. We glorify God by honoring the holiest of His children — and the greatest honor we can give the saints is that of allowing their pilgrimage of faith to guide us on our own journey home.

January

January 2 — St. Basil the Great (Bishop and Doctor)

The bishop and theologian St. Basil the Great (329–379) played an important role in the Church's struggle against the heresy of *Arianism*. Basil came from an amazing family: his grandmother, father, mother, elder sister, and two younger brothers were all, like him, canonized saints. Upon being ordained a priest, Basil spent several years assisting the bishop of Caesarea (located in modern-day Turkey); in 370 he became bishop of Caesarea himself. Basil was immediately involved in the Arian controversy (the mistaken belief that Jesus was only human, and not also divine). Because he steadfastly upheld the Church's teaching, Basil encountered much opposition; the imperial family was numbered among his enemies, and Basil had little support from other Church leaders. Nonetheless, his influence was so great that, two years after his death, his teachings played a major role in resolving the Arian crisis at the Council of Constantinople. Though a great theologian, Basil was more revered by his people because of his pastoral care for their needs. The bishop preached to huge crowds twice a day, cared for the poor, and built a hospital for the sick and a shelter for visitors. Basil also found time to write many letters and books on various theological subjects. St. Basil died in 379; he is considered one of the great Doctors (an eminent and reliable teachers) of the Church.

LESSONS

1. The life of St. Basil is one of the clearest demonstrations in Church history of the importance of the family; the presence of so many holy role models was undoubtedly a profound influence upon him. One of our greatest duties as Christians is assisting the spiritual growth of our family members.

2. True greatness comes not merely from heroic deeds, but from serving the needs of others; St. Basil's influence resulted both from his defense of the faith and from addressing the needs of his people.

January 2 — St. Gregory of Nazianzus
(Priest and Theologian)

St. Gregory (329–389) was a friend of St. Basil the Great and the son of the bishop of Nazianzus (located in modern-day Turkey). Gregory received a good education; because he was sensitive and shy, he desired a secluded life as a monk; however, around the year 362, his father ordained him a priest — practically by force (for Gregory was opposed to the idea). He joined his friend Basil in a monastery until the latter was made bishop of Caesarea in 370; two years later St. Basil appointed Gregory the bishop of Sasima. Instead of going there, however, Gregory stayed at Nazianzus to help his father (which caused a temporary falling-out with St. Basil). After spending several more years in a monastery, Gregory went to Constantinople — the capital of the Eastern Empire. The Arian controversy (which denied the divinity of Christ) was coming to an end, and Gregory's preaching on the Holy Trinity did much to strengthen the true faith in the imperial city. In 380, Gregory — because his eloquence had helped rebuild the Christian community in Constantinople — was chosen bishop of the city; due to the controversies and difficulties he encountered, however, he resigned after a few weeks, and spent the remainder of his life in solitude and contemplation.

LESSONS

1. God is able to use people of many different talents and personalities. The two friends Basil the Great and Gregory of Nazianzus both played important roles in overcoming the heresy of Arianism, but St. Basil took a direct and forceful role, while St. Gregory preferred to remain behind the scenes.

2. The Lord's call challenges us to move beyond our weaknesses, but does not overwhelm our personalities. St. Gregory was called to serve the Church in ways that were uncomfortable or out of character for someone with a shy and sensitive nature, but he was also allowed many opportunities for his preferred lifestyle of silence and solitude.

3. St. Gregory and St. Basil had a temporary falling out, showing that even saints can be subject to misunderstandings and disagreements — but these can be resolved through Christian charity.

January 4 — St. Elizabeth Ann Seton
(Religious and Foundress)

The first American-born saint, St. Elizabeth Ann Seton (1774–1821) was born in New York City of a prominent Episcopalian family. Her mother died when she was three, and a younger sister died the following year. At the age of nineteen Elizabeth married William Magee Seton, a wealthy businessman. They had five children and lived very happily for eleven years, but then Mr. Seton's business failed and he contracted tuberculosis. Elizabeth travelled with him to Italy, hoping the climate would help him recover, but he died there. While in Italy Elizabeth was attracted to Catholicism because of the compassion of a simple Italian family, and Catholicism's belief in the Real Presence, devotion to Mary, and its historical link to Christ and the Apostles. When Elizabeth converted in 1805, many of her family and friends rejected her. In order to support her children, she opened a school in Boston. She and her co-workers lived as a religious order, and in 1809 were officially recognized as such (the origin of the Sisters of Charity). Mother Seton, as Elizabeth became known, thus established the first American religious community for women, along with the first American parish school and the first Catholic orphanage in the United States. In spite of much suffering (the deaths of two of her daughters, the waywardness of one of her sons, and long periods of spiritual dryness), Mother Seton faithfully worked among the poor and uneducated until her death on January 4, 1821.

LESSONS

1. Difficult childhood experiences can be a source of grace; the death of Elizabeth's mother and sister gave her an early awareness of the importance of preparing for the life to come.

2. Compassion to those who are suffering can be a means of convincing them of the truth of our faith.

3. As Jesus warned, the decision to follow Him may often be a source of division within families (Luke 12:52 53); St. Elizabeth Ann Seton discovered this to be true.

January 5 — St. John Neumann (Bishop)

St. John Neumann (1811–1860) was one of the first Americans to be canonized. He was born on March 20, 1811 in Bohemia (in Eastern Europe). As a young man, John had a great desire to dedicate himself to working in the American missions. After studying in Prague, he came to New York City at the age of twenty-five. He was ordained in 1836, and after four years of missionary work in New York, he joined the Congregation of the Most Holy Redeemer (the religious order known as the Redemptorists). John continued his labors as a missionary, spending most of his time in the states of Ohio, Maryland, Virginia, and Pennsylvania. At the age of forty-one John Neumann was consecrated bishop of Philadelphia. As chief shepherd of the most important American diocese, John particularly devoted himself to organizing a strong parochial school system; in a short time the number of students increased twenty-fold. (This was especially important because the public schools of the day tended to promote Protestant religious doctrines.) Bishop Neumann arranged for teaching orders of sisters and brothers to assist in this project, and he also established many new parishes to serve the needs of numerous immigrants from Europe. St. John Neumann died on January 5, 1860. He was beatified in 1963 (the final process before becoming a saint), and canonized (officially declared a saint) on June 19, 1977.

LESSONS

1. Sometimes a youthful dream actually reflects a person's call from God; St. John Neumann's lifelong desire to serve as a missionary in America was fulfilled in a holy and wonderful way.

2. A strong Catholic school system is a vital element in preserving the faith; this is especially true when the public schools oppose or undermine Catholicism — either from a Protestant perspective (as in the nineteenth century), or from a secular or humanistic one (as often happens today).

January 6 — Blessed André Bessette (Religious)

The religious brother Blessed André Bessette (1845–1937) became internationally known for his great devotion to St. Joseph and for his involvement in hundreds of miraculous cures — all of which he attributed to the intercession of the holy spouse of Mary. André was born near Montreal, the eighth of twelve children. He had a difficult childhood, being sickly and weak, and both his parents died when he was about twelve. After being adopted, André became a farmhand; he then unsuccessfully tried a number of trades, including baking, shoemaking, and blacksmithing. During the U.S. Civil War he worked in an American factory; then, at the age of twenty-five, he sought to enter the Congregation of the Holy Cross. Because of poor health, André was not at first allowed to continue past his novitiate (a period of training for the religious life), but with the help of Bishop Ignace Bourget of Montreal, he was finally admitted into the order. Brother André was given the simple and humble task of doorkeeper at Notre Dame College in Montreal, also serving as sacristan, laundry worker, and messenger. He later said, "When I joined this community, the superiors showed me the door, and I remained forty years." Every night Brother André spent hours in prayer, and his prayers and visits to the sick were reputed to work miracles; all of those under his care during an epidemic completely recovered. His superiors were suspicious, and doctors disparaged his efforts, but thousands of people sought his assistance (and eventually he needed four secretaries to handle the 80,000 letters he received each year). Thanks to Brother André's influence, a chapel in honor of St. Joseph was built on Mount Royal in Montreal, and numerous people visited him there — many of them being healed of their illnesses. When Brother André died at the age of ninety-two, thousands of residents from Montreal attended his funeral.

LESSONS

1. We do not need important positions to do great things for God's glory, but only great faith.

2. Blessed André Bessette's life was modelled on that of St. Joseph: a simple and humble man used to manual labor and hard work. We too can be blessed through the intercession of St. Joseph, especially when we imitate his desire to serve others and his example of humility.

January 7 — St. Raymond (Bishop and Religious)

St. Raymond of Peñafort (1175–1275) was a Spanish Dominican particularly noted for his work in codifying Church law. He was born into a noble family at the town of Peñafort. By age twenty he was a professor of philosophy, and in his thirties he received his doctorate in law (both Church and civil). At the age of forty-seven Raymond gave up his academic career and joined the newly-established Dominican Order. Some years after this the Pope called him to Rome and asked him to compile and organize all the decrees issued by various Popes and Church councils of the past century. Raymond's work, known as the "Decretals," served as the standard reference on canon law (Church regulations) until the twentieth century. At age sixty Raymond was appointed archbishop in the Spanish province of Aragon. He disliked the honor and authority of the position, however, and his illness two years later gave him an excuse to resign. The following year the Dominicans elected him as head of the Order. Raymond carefully fulfilled his responsibilities, visited all the Dominican establishments on foot, and revised the Order's constitution so that the Master General (the head of the Order) could be allowed to resign. When this new constitution was accepted, Raymond (then age sixty-five) promptly resigned from office. St. Raymond spent the remaining thirty-five years of his life teaching, encouraging the great Dominican scholar St. Thomas Aquinas in his writings, and opposing heresy and working for the conversion of the Moors (Moslems) in Spain. St. Raymond died at the age of 100.

LESSONS

1. A long life can be a glorious one — if it is lived in the service of God and His people.

2. Church law — though an unpopular subject with many Catholics — is necessary for the community of faith; Jesus spoke of fulfilling the law, not abolishing it (Matthew 5:17–19).

January 13 — St. Hilary (Bishop and Doctor)

St. Hilary of Poitiers (315?–368) was born of a well-to-do pagan family, and received a good education. He became a Christian after reading Scripture. At the age of thirty-five, though married, Hilary was elected bishop of his native city of Poitiers in France (clerical celibacy had not yet become mandatory). Hilary became a leading figure in the fight against the heresy of *Arianism*. Arius, after whom the heresy is named, was a priest who taught that Jesus was not truly divine, but only human. This heresy soon became widespread and attracted a number of powerful supporters, including many bishops and some of the Roman emperors. In Egypt Arianism was opposed by the bishop St. Athanasius, whose unyielding defense of the Church's teaching did much to preserve true Christian faith. St. Hilary was something of a Western counterpart to Athanasius (indeed, he became known as the "Athanasius of the West"). In 356 Hilary refused the emperor's order that all the bishops in Western Europe sign a condemnation of St. Athanasius, and accordingly was banished to Phrygia, an Arian stronghold (located in modern-day Turkey). Even in exile he continued to oppose Arianism in his writing and preaching. When Hilary demanded a public debate with the local Arian bishop, the heretics — fearing the outcome — begged the emperor to remove him as a troublemaker — and so he was returned to Poitiers. Hilary continued to oppose Arianism, though he was gentle and forgiving with the heretics themselves, and he tried to reconcile those who had accepted Arianism through ignorance or fear. St. Hilary died in 368, and was later declared a Doctor (an eminent and reliable teacher) of the Church.

LESSONS

1. Sometimes religious truth is unpopular or "politically incorrect," yet it remains true — and Christians have a duty of standing up for it, as did St. Hilary (and also St. Athanasius).

2. We must be fierce in defending the truth, but gentle in our dealings with those who oppose it; St. Hilary uncompromisingly opposed Arianism, but was forgiving toward the Arians themselves.

January 17 — St. Anthony of Egypt (Abbot)

The famous abbot and hermit of the Egyptian desert, St. Anthony (251–356) was raised as a Christian; when his parents died, he inherited their estate. At the age of twenty he heard Christ's words in the Gospel, "Go, sell what you have and give it to the poor." Profoundly moved, Anthony did this; after arranging for the care of his younger sister, he went into the desert for a life of solitude and prayer. He experienced numerous physical and spiritual temptations — including fierce demonic assaults — but overcame them, and soon developed a reputation for holiness. Many people came to him for advice, and even the great Emperor Constantine wrote to him, asking for prayers. Anthony eventually established a sort of monastery of scattered cells, and occasionally visited his followers during his later years. He sought to be martyred during a Roman persecution in 311, but this was denied him; he was later very active in opposing the Arian heresy (which denied Christ's divinity). St. Anthony lived to be over 100, and is often considered the founder of *monasticism* (the lifestyle practiced by hermits and monks); his life was recorded by his friend and disciple St. Athanasius, who wrote his biography in *The Life of St. Anthony*.

LESSONS

1. Though we may not be called to give away all our money and possessions, as did St. Anthony, we must avoid being possessed by them; unlike the rich young man (Matthew 19:16–24), we must be willing to place God's call ahead of any material considerations.

2. Evil spirits sometimes try to prevent a person's growth in holiness, but those who persevere will — through the help of God's grace — prevail.

3. Even though we might desire to serve God in a glorious way, this may not be His plan for us; St. Anthony's desire for martyrdom, noble as it was, was not fulfilled.

January 20 — St. Fabian (Pope and Martyr)

The twentieth pope in the Church's history, St. Fabian was an unlikely but inspired choice. In 236 Pope St. Anterus died after a reign of just over a month. Fabian was a Christian layman who owned a farm outside Rome; he happened to come into the city as the clergy and laity were about to elect a new Pope. According to the great church historian Eusebius, a blue dove suddenly came down from Heaven and settled on Fabian's head. Interpreting this as a sign from God, the people unanimously elected Fabian as Bishop of Rome. He served as Pope for the next fourteen years, ruling with wisdom and firmness; under his leadership, the Church in Rome grew to perhaps 40,000 persons. It was Fabian who first erected buildings at area cemeteries; these were built for the convenience of Christians who, modifying the pagan practice of holding memorial feasts at the graves of loved ones, began celebrating and praying at the burial sites of early martyrs. Pope Fabian had a strong personality; an African bishop claimed that the pagan Roman Emperor Decius would have sooner chosen to cope with a political rival than with the Bishop of Rome. Thus, when Decius ordered an empire-wide persecution of the Church in 250, he made sure Fabian was among the first to be killed.

LESSONS

1. There are times when God uses direct signs to indicate His will, and those who act in accord with it are blessed. St. Fabian was a surprise choice for pope, but the Church prospered during his reign.

2. The Church will sometimes legitimately borrow customs from the secular world, adapting them to her own use; the pagan practice of remembering the dead also served Christian purposes, and St. Fabian was willing to acknowledge this.

January 20 — St. Sebastian (Martyr)

St. Sebastian (257?–288) was a third century martyr for Christ. Little is known about his life, though there are a number of popular legends about him. Sebastian was a Roman martyr; he was buried by the Appian Way (a major road) outside Rome, and devotion to him began at an early date. Aside from that, nothing is historically certain. Legends about St. Sebastian claim that he was a Roman soldier who secretly devoted himself to aiding Christians who had been condemned to death. When his own adherence to Christianity was discovered, he was sentenced to death and imprisoned. Two other Christians in prison were on the verge of abandoning their religion so as to save their lives, but Sebastian's impassioned speech to them not only reinforced their faith, but also converted several others who heard him. The legend of St. Sebastian's death states that he was tied to a tree and shot with arrows, but somehow survived. Upon recovery, he refused to flee for safety, but instead sought out the emperor and criticized him for ordering a persecution of Christians. Recovering from his shock, the emperor supposedly then ordered Sebastian seized and beaten to death with clubs. St. Sebastian was soon venerated by Christians, especially in Milan, and the legends which grew up about him served as the subjects of many Renaissance paintings.

LESSONS

1. Colorful legends often round out the few known historical facts about the early saints, but this is not necessarily a drawback; God's truth — in this case, that divine strength can help us remain faithful even unto death — can be conveyed not only through verifiable biographies, but also through embellished stories and popular devotions.

2. Followers of Christ face many obstacles and temptations in their struggle to remain faithful, and — as shown by the legend of St. Sebastian — the firm support of a fellow Christian can be crucial to their success. Our efforts to encourage other believers can thus be of immense value.

3. As Jesus said, "No one has greater love than this, to lay down one's life for one's friends" (John 15:13). By dying as a martyr, St. Sebastian proved himself to be a true friend of Christ.

January 21 — St. Agnes (Virgin and Martyr)

The virgin and martyr St. Agnes is one of the most famous Roman martyrs, but very little is actually known about her; for instance, scholars disagree on whether she died during the persecution of the Emperor Valerian in 258 or of the Emperor Diocletian in 304. According to legend, Agnes, a girl of twelve or thirteen, had many suitors, but refused to marry because she had vowed herself to virginity. One of the young men, in his disappointment, denounced her as a Christian. Agnes was arrested and confined to a house of prostitution. There, according to the legend, a man who looked upon her with lust lost his sight — though it was restored through her prayer. Agnes was condemned to death and executed by being stabbed in the throat; she was buried near Rome in a catacomb that was eventually named after her. The great bishop St. Ambrose, writing of St. Agnes' feast, said, "This is a virgin's birthday; let us follow her example of chastity. It is a martyr's birthday; let us offer sacrifices; it is the birthday of holy Agnes; let men be filled with wonder, little ones with hope, married women with awe and the unmarried with emulation. It seems to me that this child, holy beyond human nature, received the name Agnes [the Greek word for 'pure'] not as an earthly designation but as a revelation from God of what she was to be."

LESSONS

1. St. Agnes was like one of the wise virgins found ready for her Master's coming (cf. Matthew 25:1–13); like her, we must be willing to renounce all things for Christ's glory.

2. Jesus tells us, "love your enemies and pray for those who persecute you" (Matthew 5:44); according to legend, St. Agnes did this by praying for the man whose sight was lost.

3. Purity and holiness go hand-in-hand; to be true followers of Jesus, we must strive to remain chaste.

January 22 — St. Vincent (Deacon and Martyr)

St. Vincent was a deacon who suffered martyrdom early in the fourth century. He lived in Spain and was ordained a deacon by St. Valerius, the bishop of Saragossa. In 303, edicts were published against the Christian clergy, and in the following year these were extended to the laity as well. Vincent and Bishop Valerius were imprisoned in the city of Valencia, where they suffered from hunger and from torture, administered by a local official named Dacian. Vincent and Valerius would not renounce their faith; they only seemed to grow stronger under their sufferings. Dacian sent Valerius into exile and devoted all his efforts to breaking Vincent. Many different tortures were inflicted upon him, but to no avail; indeed, they had a greater effect on Dacian, who grew more and more frustrated (even to the point of having the torturers themselves beaten because they had failed). Dacian tried a different tactic, promising to release Vincent if only he would hand over the Church's books to be burnt. Vincent refused, and after still further torture, was tossed into a filthy cell — where he managed to convert the jailer. Dacian wept with rage; perhaps realizing that he was beaten, he then allowed Vincent's friends to visit him. When they lovingly placed him upon a comfortable bed, Vincent died peacefully, thereby earning the martyr's crown of glory. Devotion to St. Vincent was soon widespread, and he became the most celebrated of the Spanish martyrs.

LESSONS

1. God's strength makes it possible for us to endure far more than we would ever imagine possible; Dacian's most determined efforts failed to shake St. Vincent's faith.

2. Even under the most difficult circumstances, we are given opportunities to share the Gospel; St. Vincent's words and example converted one of those who had been persecuting him.

3. When direct assaults fail to overcome our faith, evil-doers sometimes suggest a compromise; like St. Vincent, we must be firm in rejecting anything that dilutes our adherence to Christ.

January 24 — St. Francis de Sales (Bishop)

The great bishop St. Francis de Sales (1567–1622) is known today for his gentleness and deep spirituality. His father was a senator from the province of Savoy in France, and he wanted Francis to become a lawyer and eventually take his place; to this end, Francis was sent to the University of Padua to study law. After receiving his doctorate, Francis returned home and horrified his father by announcing his desire to become a priest. After a long period of gentle but persistent urging on Francis' part, his father finally agreed, and Francis was ordained in 1593. His first assignment was to the region of Chablis in Switzerland. Though it was a stronghold of the Calvinists (Protestant followers of John Calvin), Francis' ministry was remarkably successful; he preached and wrote pamphlets explaining the Church's teaching in simple language, doing much to counteract the hatred of Catholicism which had developed following the Protestant Reformation. At the age of thirty-five he became bishop of Geneva, where he worked tirelessly to strengthen and reform the Church, in spite of many difficulties. In 1604 he met St. Jane Frances de Chantal, and six years later they mutually founded the Sisters of the Visitation. Francis was a great spiritual advisor, and his books *Introduction to the Devout Life* and *The Love of God* are still widely used. He emphasized very strongly the call to holiness which all Christians possess, stating that sanctity must be a part of daily life, regardless of one's profession. Francis himself was known for his gentle nature (though he once claimed that it took twenty years before he learned to control his temper). St. Francis died in 1622, and is considered a Doctor (an eminent and reliable teacher) of the Church.

LESSONS

1. Sometimes Christians must be bold, but quite often they can achieve great things through gentleness and persistence; St. Francis de Sales converted many Protestants back to Catholicism not by attacking their religious beliefs, but by lovingly bearing witness to the truths of the Church. As he often said, "A spoonful of honey attracts more flies than a barrelful of vinegar."

2. Our greatest faults can become provide the greatest opportunity for developing virtue; learning to control his fierce temper allowed St. Francis to become known for his gentleness and patience.

January 26 — Saints Timothy and Titus (Bishops)

Saints Timothy and Titus were companions to St. Paul and bishops in the first-century Church. Timothy was born in Lystra (a city in modern-day Turkey); his grandmother Lois had been converted by Paul, and around the year 47 Timothy and his mother Eunice also became Christians. As he matured, Timothy began assisting Paul in his missionary activities (Acts 16:1–4), carrying messages, serving as Paul's delegate to different Christian communities, and eventually becoming the first bishop of Ephesus. Two of the New Testament epistles were addressed to Timothy, and St. Paul refers to him in several of his letters. According to a legend, St. Timothy was beaten to death by a mob in 97 for opposing the observance of a pagan festival. St. Titus, a Greek from Antioch, was a close friend and disciple of St. Paul; like Timothy, he was deeply involved in Paul's missionary activities. It was Titus who carried Paul's severe letter of correction to the Corinthians, helping reconcile them to the apostle (2 Corinthians 7:5–6); eventually he was appointed by Paul to help organize the newly-founded church on the island of Crete. St. Titus died about the year 94.

LESSONS

1. Young people can have much to offer to the Church; as St. Paul wrote to Timothy, "Let no one have contempt for your youth, but set an example for those who believe" (1 Timothy 4:12). Ministry within the Church is based not on one's age, but on one's calling from God.

2. Christians are called to be agents of reconciliation, not contention; as St. Paul wrote to Titus, "Avoid foolish arguments, genealogies, rivalries, and quarrels about the law, for they are useless and futile" (Titus 3:9). We witness to the truth of the Gospel not primarily through eloquent words, but through giving a faithful example.

January 27 — St. Angela Merici
(Virgin and Foundress)

St. Angela Merici (1474–1540) was an Italian virgin and foundress of the Order of St. Ursula (the Ursuline Sisters). Angela was orphaned early in life; after joining the Third Order of St. Francis as a young woman, she devoted herself to teaching religion to children of families too poor to afford an education. Her loving dedication and charming manner made her very successful, and in 1516 she was invited to teach in the town of Brescia. On one occasion she and some companions, who shared her life of poverty and simplicity, set out on a pilgrimage to the Holy Land. Stopping on the island of Crete, Angela was struck with blindness, but she insisted on continuing, and she visited the shrines with great devotion, though she couldn't see them; on the return trip, while praying, her sight was restored in the exact place where earlier it had been lost. In 1535 Angela and her companions formally vowed themselves to the service of God, particularly the religious education of girls. The Order of St. Ursula (named after the medieval patroness of universities) didn't have formal vows or a religious habit at first; these things developed after Angela's death. The idea of a teaching order of women was new, and Angela was ahead of her time in some of her other ideas about the role of women, but she persevered and successfully led her order for the few remaining years of her life.

LESSONS

1. As St. Angela showed, the religious education of children — a vital part of the Church's mission — is most ef-

fective when the students are aware of their teachers' genuine love and respect for them.

2. What we see with our souls is more important than
what we see with our eyes; St. Angela didn't let her temporary blindness keep her from having a deep spiritual experience in the Holy Land.

January 28 — St. Thomas Aquinas
(Priest and Doctor)

The great theologian St. Thomas Aquinas (1225–1274)
was one of the most influential scholars in the Church's
history. Thomas was one of many children of a nobleman
in northern Italy. At the age of five he was sent to the
great Benedictine monastery of Monte Cassino; his parents hoped he would become a member of the respected
and relatively-prosperous Order of St. Benedict. In 1239
Thomas was sent to the University of Naples to complete
his studies, where he was attracted by the writings of the
Greek philosopher Aristotle. Four years later he joined the
newly-formed mendicant (begging) Order of St. Dominic,
much to his family's horror. At his mother's command,
Thomas was kidnapped and imprisoned for a year by one
of his brothers, but he refused to change his mind. When
finally released, Thomas went to Paris and then to Cologne,
where he studied under the Dominican scholar St. Albert
the Great. After this, he held several professorships in Paris,
lived for a time in the papal court, and directed the Dominican school in Rome. Most of his time was devoted to
preaching, teaching, and especially writing. In his writings
Thomas stressed the unity of reason and faith; he saw the

ability to think as a divine gift to be used and cherished. In addition to his profound writings and hymns on the Eucharist, Thomas is known for "baptizing" Aristotle by reinterpreting his works in the light of Christian faith and revelation. His greatest work was the *Summa Theologica*, which he intended as an exposition of the whole of Catholic theology. He never finished it, however, for after a vision granted to him while saying Mass one day in 1273, he said, "All that I have written seems to me like so much straw compared to what I have seen and what has been revealed to me." St. Thomas Aquinas died in 1274, and in 1567 Pope St. Pius V declared him to be a Doctor (an eminent and reliable teacher) of the Church.

LESSONS

1. It was said of St. Thomas Aquinas that "His wonderful learning owes far less to his genius than to the effectiveness of his prayer." Time spent in prayer is not "wasted," for in addition to glorifying God, it helps us to use His gifts and to serve Him more effectively.

2. As St. Thomas knew, faith and reason are not opposed, for God is the source of both — and He never contradicts Himself. Therefore, science and learning are never capable of "disproving" Christianity.

January 31 — St. John Bosco (Priest and Founder)

Known as the "Apostle of Youth," the Italian priest St. John Bosco (1815–1888) was born of a peasant family and raised by his widowed mother. From an early age he desired to serve God by working with boys — many of whom would today be considered juvenile delinquents. After being ordained a priest in 1841, John began his ministry to youth near the city of Turin. Encountering a poor orphan, John attended to the boy's material needs, and then instructed him for his First Communion. From this small beginning, he soon involved himself in unceasing activity for orphans and neglected youths; with his mother as a housekeeper, he opened a boarding-house for boys, taught them catechism, and provided workshops where they learned tailoring, shoemaking, and other occupations. By 1854 this ministry had expanded so much that John established a religious order to work with youths; he called this order the Salesians, after the great bishop St. Francis de Sales, whom he deeply admired. When asked what sort of habit he desired for his order, John replied, "The habit of virtue." The saint also established, with the help of St. Mary Mazzarello (a peasant woman from Genoa) the Daughters of Mary, Help of Christians, to work with girls. Even with the assistance of wealthy patrons, finances were often a problem; nevertheless, John responded to every warning of financial difficulty with a smiling assurance that "God will provide." St. John's work was not universally admired; some of the professional educators of his day felt he was much too lenient and trusting of his charges, and others claimed that a man who attempted to care for so many boys without any substantial monetary resources was obviously insane. John's boys themselves, however, were completely devoted to him. (It's said that one of them, while working in a factory, saw John passing by on the street; the boy was so eager to be with him that, instead of taking the time to open the shop door, he plunged right through it, glass pane and all.) The most famous of St. John's boys

was St. Dominic Savio, who died at the young age of fifteen; under John's influence, Dominic achieved a remarkable degree of sanctity in a few short years. John believed
all Christians are called to such holiness, and his work with
youth manifested the importance of Christian love (and so
great was the influence of this love that he himself never
recalled having formally to punish a boy). John sought to
make all things — whether they involved religion or work
— as attractive as possible for his boys; he felt his methods
were preventive, rather than oppressive, for keeping them
busy and interested in various activities would help them
overcome temptation. St. John Bosco died in 1888, and was
canonized in 1934; today the Salesian Order operates general schools, trade and agricultural schools, and hospitals
and foreign missions, throughout the world.

LESSONS

1. Jesus said, "Let the children come to Me; do not prevent them, for the kingdom of God belongs to such as
these" (Mark 10:14). As St. John Bosco recognized, children and young people are very important in Our Lord's
plan, and showing practical concern for their needs is an
important way of helping build up the Body of Christ.

2. Family members can often play a direct and important role in our own ministry; John Bosco's mother not
only gave him a deep love for God, but later also assisted
in his mission to neglected boys.

3. As the saying goes, "Idleness is the devil's workshop."
St. John knew the importance of having safe and enjoy-
able activities available for young people, so as to help them
avoid trouble and sin.

4. Money helps make the Church's mission possible, and St. John Bosco was grateful to his financial benefactors; however, trusting in God is always infinitely more important, for as Jesus said, "Ask, and it will be given you; seek and you will find; knock and the door will be opened to you" (Matthew 7:7).

February

February 3 — St. Ansgar (Missionary and Bishop)

The first missionary to Scandinavia was St. Ansgar (801–865). He was born of a noble family near Amiens in France, and became a Benedictine monk at the monastery of Corbie in Germany. In 826 Ansgar went to Denmark, whose king was a new convert to Christianity. He established a school in Schleswig, but was driven out by local pagans. The land of Sweden had asked for Christian missionaries, so Ansgar journeyed there (being captured for a time by pirates while on the way). He built the first Christian church in Sweden, and was generally successful in his missionary efforts, but in 831 he was consecrated archbishop of Hamburg in Germany. Ansgar labored there for thirteen years, only to see the city destroyed by invading Norsemen. He again returned to Denmark and Sweden, but the progress he made there lasted only during his lifetime; after his death these countries reverted to paganism (a situation which lasted for the following two centuries). In 848 Ansgar became bishop of the German city of Bremen; he spent the remainder of his life there, and developed a reputation as both a brilliant preacher and a humble and caring pastor. He performed a number of miracles in the course of his ministry; when one of his assistants boasted about this, Ansgar rebuked him and said, "If I were worthy of such a favor from God, I would ask that He grant this one miracle: that by His grace He would make of me a good man." St. Ansgar had hoped to die as a martyr, but instead he died peacefully at Bremen in 865; he is today considered the "Apostle of the North."

LESSONS

1. God measures success differently than the world does. Because St. Ansgar's missionary successes disappeared after his death, the world might judge his efforts a failure; those who see through eyes of faith, however, will realize the infinite value of the many persons who accepted the Gospel through Ansgar's preaching and ministry.

2. The virtue of humility is constantly needed, even by saints; Ansgar understood and agreed with St. Paul's words, "may I never boast except in the cross of our Lord Jesus Christ" (Galatians 6:14).

3. Not all desires are granted by God; St. Ansgar was unable to die as he wished as a martyr.

February 3 — St. Blase (Bishop and Martyr)

St. Blase was a bishop and martyr in the early fourth century. He is said to have studied philosophy as a young man, and later to have become a physician. Blase became the bishop of Sebastea in modern-day Armenia, where he was beheaded for his faith in 316. The *Acts of St. Blase* — an account of his life of questionable accuracy — was written over 400 years later; according to its legends, Blase fled to the wilderness during a time of persecution. He lived as a hermit, but made friends with the wild animals; some time after this, hunters discovered him kneeling in prayer —

surrounded by respectful lions, wolves, and bears. Legends further state that as the hunters were taking Blase to the authorities, a mother cried to him for help, for her son was choking to death on a fish bone caught in his throat. When Blase blessed the boy, the child was able to cough up the bone. (This is the origin of the custom of blessing throats on the feast of St. Blase.) Though such stories about Blase cannot be historically verified, it is known that devotion to him spread rapidly, particularly after the writing of the *Acts of St. Blase.*

LESSONS

1. Just as St. Blase showed concern for a child in need even as he himself was being arrested, so we as Christians must continue to care for others even during our own trials and difficulties.

2. The Blessing of St. Blase (*"Through the merits and intercession of St. Blase, Bishop and Martyr, may God deliver you from all diseases of the throat, and from every other evil, in the Name of the Father, and of the Son, and of the Holy Spirit"*) shows that God is concerned not only with our spiritual growth, but also with our physical needs and the demands of our daily lives.

February 5 — St. Agatha (Virgin and Martyr)

St. Agatha was a virgin and martyr of the third century. She lived in the town of Catania in Sicily, and was martyred for her Christian faith in 251 during the persecution of the Emperor Decius. Prior to this, Christians had been persecuted and martyred in various provinces of the Roman Empire, but no systematic persecution of the Church occurred until Decius instituted one in 250–251. Many legends grew up about St. Agatha, including one in the sixth century which said that she was courted by a Roman senator named Quintanius. When she rejected him, the senator denounced her as a Christian and had her arrested. Agatha prayed, "Jesus Christ, Lord of all things, You see my heart; You know my desires. Possess all that I am — You alone. I am Your sheep; make me worthy to overcome the devil." She was then turned over to an evil woman, who mistreated her and tried to corrupt her. When this failed, Agatha was arrested and tortured — though it's said that St. Peter appeared to her in a vision and strengthened her; eventually, however, she died as a result of her sufferings. The year after her death, her intercession was credited with ending a volcanic eruption of Mt. Etna, and so she is invoked against earthquakes. Devotion to St. Agatha began among the Christians of Sicily soon after her death, and she is today considered the patroness of nurses and foundrymen.

LESSONS

1. It is our human tendency to respond immediately to danger or crisis by worrying or becoming fearful. St. Agatha, however — if the legend is accurate — unhesitatingly turned to Jesus in prayer upon being arrested. Prayer should also be our first impulse in times of need or distress.

2. As with all the martyrs in the Church's history, Agatha found strength in Christ. Just as the Lord made it possible for a young woman to bear great suffering, so He will help us bear our own crosses.

February 6 — St. Paul Miki and Companions (Martyrs)

St. Paul Miki (1565?–1597) and his companions were martyred in Japan at the end of the sixteenth century. A native Japanese, Paul entered the Society of Jesus (the Jesuits) as a young man. He worked as a missionary brother, along with St. Leo Karasuma (a Korean layman), and six Franciscan missionaries from Europe, led by St. Peter Baptist of Spain. Building on the earlier work of St. Francis Xavier [December 3], the missionaries preached the Gospel around the city of Nagasaki, and were initially very successful. However, the captain of a visiting Spanish ship foolishly (and falsely) boasted that the missionaries' efforts were paving the way for a Spanish and Portuguese invasion of Japan. The Japanese shogun (warlord) Hideyoshi, already jealous of the missionaries' success, used this as an excuse to begin a severe attack on all foreign influences, including Christianity. Many Christians were martyred, including Paul Miki, John Goto, and James Kisai of Japan; Peter Baptist, Martin de Aguirre, Francis Blanco, and Francis-of-St. Michael of Spain; Philip de las Casas of Mexico; Gonsola Garcia of India, and seventeen Japanese lay people. These were all crucified and pierced with a lance. While hanging on the cross, Paul Miki spoke to the Japanese gathered below: "As I come to this supreme moment of my life, I am sure none of you would suppose I want to deceive you. And so I tell you plainly: there is no way to be saved except the Christian way. My religion teaches me to pardon my enemies and all who have offended me. I do gladly pardon the Emperor and all who have sought my death. I beg them to seek baptism and be Christians themselves."

LESSONS

1. Human boasting and political maneuvering can seem to complicate the Church's mission, as happened with the Spanish captain and the Japanese warlord; however, the example of the Christian martyrs inspired and sustained the Japanese Catholics (and when Christian missionaries returned to Japan in the nineteenth century, they found a secret community of several thousand Christians still in existence).

2. As St. Paul Miki stated while on his cross, we are called to forgive our enemies; our willingness to do this is a powerful testimony to the truth of our faith.

February 8 — St. Jerome Emiliani (Priest and Founder)

Born in Venice, St. Jerome Emiliani (1481–1537) was a soldier who lived an irreligious life. However, a fortress under his command was captured by the enemy, and he was imprisoned in a dungeon. In his hour of need, Jerome turned to God; he offered up his sufferings, spent long hours in prayer, and — through what some considered a miracle — managed to escape. Jerome returned to Venice; he began educating his nephews while undergoing his own studies for the priesthood. After he was ordained, northern Italy was ravaged by plague and famine. Jerome devoted himself to caring for the sick; he also fed the hungry at his own expense. St. Jerome made a particular point of caring for abandoned orphans; he rented a house, where he fed and clothed them, in addition to teaching them religion. (It is said that Jerome was the first to teach the catechism in a question-and-answer format.) He also established other orphanages and a hospital. In 1532, after recovering from the plague, Jerome and two other priests established a religious order known as the Clerks Regular of Somascha for the care of orphans. St. Jerome died in 1537 from an infectious disease caught while caring for the sick; in 1928 Pope Pius XI named him the patron of orphans and abandoned children.

LESSONS

1. God sometimes uses misfortune to get our attention; St. Jerome paid no attention to Him until he was defeated in war and cast into prison. This proved to be the turning point of his life.

2. St. Jerome realized that it does little good to preach the Gospel to the hungry and homeless unless practical steps are taken to alleviate their suffering; only then will the Gospel become real to them.

February 10 — St. Scholastica
(Virgin and Foundress)

St. Scholastica (480–543) was the twin sister of St. Benedict, the founder of the Benedictine Order. Benedict and Scholastica were born of wealthy parents in fifth century Italy; they were raised together until Benedict left for Rome to continue his studies. Scholastica was dedicated to God at an early age, though for a time she probably continued to stay with her parents. Some years later she left home and founded a religious order for women near Monte Cassino in central Italy, where Benedict had established his famous monastery. The twins used to visit each other once a year; since Scholastica, as a woman, was not allowed inside the monastery, their meetings occurred in a nearby farmhouse. During these occasions Benedict and his sister spent hours discussing spiritual matters. On the last of these meetings, Scholastica implored her brother to stay the entire night with her, so that they could continue talking until morning about the joys of Heaven. Benedict refused, since that would mean he and the monks accompanying him would have to break his rule about not spending a night outside the monastery. Scholastica thereupon prayed, asking God that her brother might remain. In response to her prayer, a severe thunderstorm suddenly broke out, preventing the monks from leaving. Benedict cried out, "God forgive you, sister! What have you done?" Scholastica answered, "I asked a favor of you and you refused. I asked it of God and He granted it." Benedict and Scholastica thus spent the night discussing the nature of Heaven — a fitting subject, for Scholastica was soon to experience its joys. Three days after this conversation Benedict was at prayer in his monastery when he saw the soul of his sister ascending to Heaven in the form of a dove. Benedict then announced her death to his monks, and later buried her in the tomb he had prepared for himself.

LESSONS

1. Sibling rivalry — while a very common condition in many families — is not supposed to prevent spiritual growth; just as parents are supposed to help their children grow in holiness, so brothers and sisters are meant to be a good influence upon one another.

2. When her brother denied her request, St. Scholastica was confident enough to turn to God in prayer; she recalled Jesus' words, "Ask and it will be given to you; seek and you will find; knock and the door will be opened to you" (Matthew 7:7).

February 14 — Saints Cyril and Methodius (Missionaries; Monk and Bishop)

St. Cyril (827?–869) and St. Methodius (815?–885) were brothers who became famous as missionaries to the Slavic peoples of southeastern Europe. They were born in Greece, where their father served as an army officer in the Byzantine Empire. Cyril became a brilliant instructor at the imperial university in Constantinople, and Methodius served as governor of one of the Empire's provinces. After some years, however, Methodius withdrew to a monastery. Cyril was offered the chance to take his brother's place, but instead he followed his example and also became a monk. Early in the 860s the Duke of Moravia asked the Emperor for political and religious independence from German rule, and this request — in spite of German opposition — was granted. Cyril and Methodius were sent to recruit local (non-Germanic) clergy and to establish a Slavonic liturgy. Cyril invented a Slavonic alphabet (possibly the source of the modern Russian alphabet), and he and his brother translated much of the Bible into Slavonic. Their great success as missionaries provoked envy and opposition from German religious and political authorities. When the local German bishop refused to consecrate Slavic clergy, the brothers travelled to Rome in 869 and appealed to Pope Adrian II. The Pope upheld their authority and approved their liturgy; soon after this St. Cyril, who had long been ill, died, Methodius was consecrated a bishop by the Pope, and he spent the remaining years of his life in missionary activity, despite the continued opposition of his German colleagues. At one point he was forced into exile, and he was later summoned to Rome to defend himself against his opponents' accusations. St. Methodius died in 885; he and St. Cyril are today honored by Catholics throughout southeastern Europe.

LESSONS

1. Saints Cyril and Methodius represent the Church's recognition of the importance and uniqueness of individual cultures; God is able to speak through every language and to every people.

2. Human jealousy can hinder and delay missionary activity, but not prevent it; as St. Paul noted, "There is no chaining of the word of God" (2 Timothy 2:9).

February 17 — Seven Founders of the Order of Servites (Religious)

In 1240 seven noblemen of the prosperous and cultured Italian city of Florence decided to exchange the bustle of city life for a simple lifestyle of prayer, penance, and service of God. It is said that the Virgin Mary appeared to Bonfiglio Monaldo, Bonaiunta Manetto, Manetto Antellese, Amedeo Amedei, Uguccione Uguccioni, Sosteneo Sostenei, and Alessio Falconieri, urging them to devote themselves to her service. Upon making arrangements for their families (for two of the seven were married, and two others were widowers), the men established themselves near the city. However, their solitude was disturbed by constant visitors from Florence, so they withdrew to the slopes of Mt. Senario and established a community there. In 1244 the group adopted a religious habit and chose to live under the rule of St. Augustine; at the same time, they named themselves the "Servants of Mary" (or "Servites"). Instead of choosing a more traditional form of monastic life, the original group and its newer members developed as mendicant (begging) friars, actively involving themselves in serving others and caring for the poor. The Order's first leader was St. Bonfiglio Monaldo, who died in 1261; the best known was St. Alessio Falconieri, who helped establish a Servite community in Siena and in other cities. He outlived the other founders, and is said to have been 110 when he died. The Servite Order continues to be active in caring for the poor today.

LESSONS

1. Fellowship and mutual support can be an important part of life for Christian men, and the existence of such contemporary groups as Promise Keepers and St. Joseph's Covenant Keepers emphasizes the need for male faith support networks or groups in today's society.

2. As the Seven Servites discovered, holiness involves a combination of time with God (prayer and solitude) and time with one's neighbor (community and service).

February 21 — St. Peter Damian (Bishop and Doctor)

The medieval Italian bishop St. Peter Damian (1007–1072) was born in Ravenna, where his parents died when he was still young. Peter was first left with an older brother, who was very unkind and neglectful; later another brother cared for him, and arranged for him to be well-educated. Peter became a professor, and in 1035 he joined the Benedictine Order. Peter soon gained a reputation for being generous to the poor; it was his custom to invite one or two poor persons to share his meals. In the monastery Peter practiced severe penances, going long periods without food or sleep, and spending hours in prayer. Eventually Peter became abbot of the monastery, and devoted himself to fostering spiritual reform and renewal. The pope frequently asked him to mediate in disputes involving different monasteries or disagreements between local religious and government officials. Peter was then appointed bishop of Ostia (the port city of Rome), where he was vigorous in his efforts at reform; he restored discipline among his clergy and promoted a simpler and more spiritual lifestyle for his people. He wrote many letters and sermons, but throughout this period he desired to return to the monastic life. This request was finally granted, but he was still called to serve as a papal legate from time to time. After returning from one such assignment, Peter was overcome by a fever. With his monks gathered around him in prayer, St. Peter Damian died on February 22, 1072; in 1828 he was declared a Doctor (an eminent and reliable teacher) of the Church.

LESSONS

1. Personal experiences of suffering should make us sympathetic to others in need; St. Peter's difficult childhood made him particularly mindful of the poor and lowly.

2. Holiness requires us to be both firm and gentle. St. Peter had a reputation for being quite impatient and critical with those who took religion casually, but he could also be very consoling and encouraging to those experiencing difficulty or sorrow.

February 23 — St. Polycarp (Bishop and Martyr)

St. Polycarp was a second century bishop and martyr, and an important leader in the early Church. He became a Christian while very young, and was a disciple of St. John the Apostle and a friend of St. Ignatius of Antioch. St. John appointed Polycarp as bishop of Smyrna (in modern-day Turkey), and St. Ignatius visited him there while on his way to Rome (where he was to be martyred). As a leader of the eastern Church, Polycarp himself travelled to Rome to discuss with Pope Anicetus the proper date of Easter; it was agreed that East and West would continue their customs of celebrating Easter on different dates. Polycarp wrote several epistles; only his *Letter to the Philippians* still exists. *The Acts of Polycarp* was written by Christians in Smyrna soon after his death about the year 156, and — with the exception of the account of St. Stephen's death in *The Acts of the Apostles* — is the oldest existing factual account of an early Christian's martyrdom. According to the story, Polycarp was betrayed by a servant, arrested, and led before the proconsul and a crowd that had gathered in the stadium. Upon being ordered to curse Christ, the bishop responded, "I have served Him for eighty-six years and He has done me no wrong. How can I blaspheme my King and Savior?" The proconsul, at the urging of the crowd, thereupon ordered him burnt at the stake. Polycarp praised God amid the flames, which miraculously failed to touch him, so he was instead killed by a spear thrust at the proconsul's orders (and according to legend, so much of his blood flowed that the flames were extinguished).

LESSON

1. In his *Letter to the Philippians*, St. Polycarp wrote: "Stand fast, therefore, in this conduct and follow the example of the Lord, 'firm and unchangeable in faith, lovers of the brotherhood, loving each other, united in truth,' helping each other with the mildness of the Lord, despising no one." The holy bishop himself followed his advice to be both gentle and strong.

2. Like Polycarp, we are called to remain true to Christ, for He has always been true to us.

March

March 3 — Blessed Katherine Drexel
(Virgin and Religious)

Blessed Katherine Drexel (1858–1955) was an American heiress who gave up a fortune in order to serve native Americans and blacks. She was born in Philadelphia to a wealthy and religious family, and from an early age her parents' example encouraged her own concern for the poor. After nursing her stepmother through a long illness, Katherine realized that wealth could not preserve one from suffering and death. During a European tour, when young Katherine met Pope Leo XIII and asked him to send more missionaries to the U.S., the Pope shocked her by saying, "Why don't *you* become a missionary?" This is what Katherine did, giving away her fortune and founding the Sisters of the Blessed Sacrament for Indians and Colored People. In 1894 Mother Drexel, as Katherine became known, opened the first mission school for Indians in New Mexico; its success quickly led to the founding of numerous other schools by her Order, including schools for native Americans west of the Mississippi River and schools for blacks in the southern U.S. One of Katherine's greatest achievements was the establishment in 1915 of Xavier University in New Orleans — the first American university for blacks. By 1942 she had a system of black Catholic schools in thirteen states, along with fifty mission schools for Indians in sixteen states — despite the opposition of segregationists (who burned one of her schools in Pennsylvania). At the age of seventy-seven Mother Drexel was forced to retire after suffering a heart attack; she spent the remaining nineteen years of her life in constant prayer and meditation.

LESSONS

1. As Jesus said, "Much will be required of the person entrusted with much" (Luke 12:48). Katherine understood this; instead of living a life of luxury and pleasure, she chose one of sacrifice and service.

2. Donating money can be a way of avoiding a personal commitment. Even though she gave away over $12 million, Katherine realized that this wasn't enough: Jesus was asking her not merely to give money, but to devote her entire life to the service of His people.

March 4 — St. Casimir (Prince)

The patron saint of Poland and Lithuania, St. Casimir (1458–1483) was the second son of King Casimir IV and third in line for the Polish throne. While a youth, Casimir was educated by the great Polish scholar John Dlugosz, from whom he learned to be virtuous and devout; he also practiced many forms of penance, and dedicated himself to a life of celibacy. In 1471 Hungarian princes became dissatisfied with their king, and sent a delegation to King Casimir, asking him to send his son to take over the country. Against the young prince's wishes, the king agreed. Casimir was sent to Hungary at the head of an army, but found that he was outnumbered by forces loyal to the Hungarian king. Accepting the advice of his officers, Casimir decided to return home without seeking battle. His father was very angry, and had Casimir imprisoned for three months. The youth, for his part, decided he would never again become involved in military affairs (and thus Casimir is considered the patron saint of conscientious objectors). From then on Casimir devoted himself to prayer and study, though he reigned briefly as king when his father was out of the country. In 1483 he withstood intense pressure to enter into a marriage with a daughter of the Holy Roman Emperor, wishing instead to maintain his vow of celibacy. Soon after this Casimir died of tuberculosis, and was buried in the Lithuanian city of Vilna, which he had been visiting at the time of his death.

LESSONS

1. Young people, with proper guidance and encouragement, are capable of making noble and heroic decisions; St. Casimir was influenced by his tutor to shun the attractions of luxury and power and to choose a life of celibacy and penance.

2. Acting on Jesus' words "What profit would a man show for gaining the whole world in exchange for his soul?" (Matthew 16:26), St. Casimir spurned military glory and power and instead chose peace.

March 7 — Saints Perpetua and Felicity (Martyrs)

Saints Perpetua and Felicity, along with several Christian companions, were put to death for their faith at the beginning of the third century. Unlike questionable legends about many of the early martyrs, an authentic account of their imprisonment and deaths was preserved, written in part by Perpetua herself (from her diary) and by another martyr, and completed after their executions by an unknown Christian. Perpetua was a young noblewoman of Carthage (a city in North Africa), the daughter of a Christian mother and a pagan father. It's believed she was a widow, for she also had an infant son. Felicity was a married slave girl, far advanced in pregnancy. The two women and three fellow catechumens — Saturninus, Secundulus, and Revocatus — had been converted to Christianity by a layman named Saturus; they were baptized while under house arrest for refusing to worship the pagan gods, and when they were transferred to the common jail, Saturus voluntarily joined them. Felicity gave birth to a girl while enduring the taunting of an unfriendly jailer; this child was adopted and raised by a fellow Christian. Perpetua was worried about her own son, who for a time she kept with her in jail, until her parents took the child home. Perpetua wrote a description of her father's visit: "When my father in his affection for me was trying to turn me from my purpose by arguments and thus weaken my faith, I said to him, 'Do you see this vessel — waterpot or whatever it may be? Can it be called by any other name than what it is?' 'No,' he replied. 'So also I cannot call myself by any other name than what I am — a Christian," Perpetua explained. The six Christians refused to renounce their faith, and all were sentenced to death during public games in the amphitheater in 203. Saints Perpetua, Felicity, and their companions were first mauled by wild animals and then put to death by the sword; it's said that the executioner was so shaken by Perpetua's brave and noble demeanor that she herself had to guide his blade to her neck.

LESSONS

1. Christians may be called upon to endure great sufferings — but if so, God will sustain them. In her diary Perpetua wrote, "What a day of horror! Terrible heat, owing to the crowds! Rough treatment by the soldiers! To crown all, I was tormented with anxiety for my baby. . . . Such anxieties I suffered for many days, but I obtained leave for my baby to remain in the prison with me, and being relieved of my trouble and anxiety for him, I at once recovered my health, and my prison became a palace to me and I would rather have been there than anywhere else."

2. Jesus said, "Whoever loves father or mother more than Me is not worthy of Me" (Matthew 10:37).

St. Perpetua showed love and respect to her father, but she did not forget her primary identity: a Christian called to follow in the footsteps of her Master.

March 8 — St. John of God (Religious)

A contemporary of St. Ignatius of Loyola [July 31], the Portuguese St. John of God (1495–1550) was also a soldier who underwent a profound conversion and who later established a religious order. At the age of forty John wanted to give his life to God, perhaps by dying as a martyr; he was instead advised to seek God by the manner in which he lived his daily life. While in Spain, John was profoundly moved by the preaching of Blessed John of Avila, and in response spent a day publicly beating himself in repentance for his sins. John was thereupon committed to a lunatic asylum, where Blessed John visited him and advised him to be more active in caring for the needs of others, instead of enduring personal hardships. This advice had a calming effect, and John went on to establish a house where he cared for the poor and the sick. His love and devotion touched many people, and benefactors aided his efforts with money and provisions. On one occasion the Archbishop of Granada summoned John because of a complaint that his hospital was open to prostitutes and tramps. John fell on his knees and said, "The Son of Man came for sinners, and we are bound to seek their conversion. I am unfaithful to my vocation because I neglect this, but I confess that I know of no bad person in my hospital except myself alone, who am indeed unworthy to eat the bread of the poor." Profoundly moved by this, the Archbishop became one of John's strongest supporters. The saint continued his efforts for another ten years, and organized the Brothers Hospitallers when his health failed. St. John died on his knees before the altar on March 8, 1550, and is considered the patron of nurses and of the sick.

LESSONS

1. Dramatic acts of penance may have their place, but as St. John was taught by Blessed John of Avila, actively

caring for the poor is more practical and often more valuable in the eyes of God.

2. Holiness and humility go hand-in-hand; St. John sincerely believed that the poor, the lowly, and even the outcasts whom he served in his hospital were worthier and more important than himself.

March 9 — St. Frances of Rome (Laywoman)

St. Frances of Rome (1384–1440) was a member of the Roman aristocracy; she wished to enter a convent, but in obedience to her parents, was instead married at age thirteen to a young nobleman named Lorenzo de' Ponziani. Frances was a good wife and household manager, and the mother of two sons and a daughter. She and her sister-in-law both desired to spend time in prayer and service to the poor; with their husbands' blessings, the two women performed various acts of faith and charity. In addition to her family responsibilities, Frances cared for victims of epidemics and wars (both of which were frequent events in fifteenth century Italy). In 1409 Lorenzo was forced into exile because of a civil war; he returned five years later as a broken man, and Frances also cared for him, in addition to her other activities. A severe plague struck Rome, claiming two of the couple's three children; Frances sold all her possessions to raise funds for caring for the sick, and then she and her sister-in-law went begging door to door for additional money. Frances organized a society of Roman women who shared her desire for self-denial and charitable works; after her husband Lorenzo died in 1436 following forty years of married life (during which, it's said, the two of them never had a quarrel), Frances spent the remainder of her life with her community.

LESSONS

1. One of the reasons obedience is valuable is that our noble aspirations aren't necessarily God's will for us. By agreeing to marriage, young St. Frances gained a husband who supported her ministry, and also received more opportunities to be of service to others than she would ever have expected.

2. Most people are called to experience holiness not in a monastery or convent, but in the responsibilities and activities of daily life. St. Frances once said, "It is most laudable in a married woman to be devout, but she must never forget that she is a housewife. And sometimes she must leave God at the altar to find Him in her housekeeping."

March 17 — St. Patrick (Missionary and Bishop)

The patron saint of Ireland, St. Patrick (389?–461) was born near the west coast of Britain, the son of a Roman civil servant. At age sixteen Patrick was carried off by Irish raiders and sold as a slave in Ireland, where he worked as a shepherd for six years. During this time he became very religious, spending long hours in prayer and meditation. Patrick finally escaped Ireland by means of a ship sailing to the European continent. He was reunited with his family in Britain, but soon returned to France to study for the priesthood; then he spent fifteen years in a monastery. A dream he had many years earlier convinced Patrick he was called to return to Ireland as a missionary, and in 432 he was consecrated a bishop and sent to preach the Gospel to the Irish people. There were some believers in Ireland, but Christianity had made few inroads there, and Patrick had many obstacles to overcome. Going to the northern and western parts of the island, which Christian missionaries had not yet reached, Patrick — with the protection of local kings — was able to make many converts. His efforts were opposed by pagan druids and even by other Christians, who criticized his methods, but Patrick's preaching bore great fruit. He ordained clergy, established dioceses, and founded several monasteries, thus preparing for the day when Ireland would virtually alone remain true to the faith and send out numerous missionaries to rechristianize Europe. In his *Confessions*, the Apostle to the Irish wrote, "I, Patrick, a sinner, am the most ignorant and of least account among the faithful, despised by many . . . I owe it to God that so many people should through me be born again to Him." St. Patrick died on March 17, 461.

LESSONS

1. Apparent misfortunes or setbacks can prove to be spiritual opportunities; St. Patrick's six years of captivity as a youth gave him the chance to develop a rich prayer life.

2. Our efforts to serve God can bear fruit many years later; the Irish missionaries who revitalized the Church during the Dark Ages can be traced back to St. Patrick's evangelizing activities.

3. Humility — which Patrick expressed in his *Confessions* — allows God to do great things through us.

March 18 — St. Cyril of Jerusalem (Bishop and Doctor)

St. Cyril (315?–386) was born of a Christian family in Jerusalem, where he received a good education. He was ordained a priest, and given the task of teaching catechumens who were preparing to be baptized at the Easter Vigil. Cyril's teachings were later collected in written form, and are important examples of the Church's ritual and theology in the fourth century. In 348 Cyril was installed as bishop of Jerusalem, and soon became involved in the Arian controversy. The heresy of *Arianism*, which denied the divinity of Jesus (and was named after a priest named Arius), spread throughout much of the Roman Empire; many bishops and clergy became Arians, and engaged in a power struggle with those who remained true to the Church's teaching. For a time the Arians were more successful, and Cyril and other orthodox bishops experienced persecution and exile. Cyril was banished three different times for refusing to accept Arian teachings (and ironically, he himself was once wrongly accused of Arian sympathies). After returning to Jerusalem following his third exile, Cyril devoted himself to restoring order and to teaching true doctrine. He participated in the Council of Constantinople in 381, which emphasized Jesus' divinity and equality with God the Father. St. Cyril died in 386, and is considered a Doctor (an eminent and reliable teacher) of the Church.

LESSONS

1. Training and welcoming new members is an important part of the Church's mission; the early catechume-

nate process, which St. Cyril was involved in, has been restored today in the R.C.I.A. (Rite of Christian Initiation for Adults).

2. A desire to serve God faithfully is no guarantee of popularity or success within the Church; Cyril experienced persecution precisely because he insisted on upholding true Christian doctrine.

March 19 — St. Joseph (Husband of Mary)

St. Joseph was the husband of Mary and the foster-father of Jesus. What little we know of his life comes from the Gospels According to Matthew and Luke. Joseph's father was named Jacob, and he was a descendant of King David (Matthew 1:16). While working as a carpenter in Nazareth, Joseph became formally engaged to Mary, being willing to respect her vow of perpetual virginity. When Mary was discovered to be pregnant, Joseph naturally assumed she had been unfaithful to him. He could have denounced her, thus sparing his reputation while ruining hers, but he didn't want to hurt her — so he decided to combine mercy and justice by divorcing her quietly. It was after Joseph made this noble decision that the angel of the Lord revealed the truth to him (Matthew 1:18–25). Joseph believed this amazing message; he went ahead with his marriage to Mary, and then took her to Bethlehem for a census; while there, Jesus was born (Luke 2:1–7). Because he was the head of the Holy Family, it was to Joseph that God sent an angel with a warning to flee to Egypt (Matthew 2:13–15); when it was safe, the Holy Family returned to Nazareth. As an upright and hard-working man, Joseph taught Jesus his own trade of carpentry, and faithfully guarded and served Him and Mary. Tradition states that St. Joseph died sometime before Jesus began His public ministry at the age of thirty; he is considered the Patron of the Universal Church and the Patron of a Happy Death.

LESSONS

1. True greatness doesn't depend on all the right "advantages": wealth, a good education, and the proper social connections. St. Joseph had none of these things, but his humility and integrity allowed God to make him one of the greatest saints.

2. Genuine humility doesn't excuse us from our responsibilities. Joseph knew he couldn't compare in holiness to Jesus or Mary — but he nonetheless exercised authority over them in accord with God's will.

March 23 — St. Turibius of Mongrovejo (Bishop)

One of the first saints of the New World, the Spanish bishop St. Turibius of Mongrovejo (1538–1606) was born in Mayorga, Spain, and educated as a lawyer. He was such a brilliant scholar that he became professor of law at the University of Salamanca. In 1580 the archbishopric of Lima, capital of Spain's colony in Peru, became vacant. Religious and political leaders agreed that Turibius' holiness made him the ideal choice for this position, even though he protested that, as a layman, he was ineligible. Turibius' protests were overruled; he was ordained a priest and bishop, and then sent to Peru. The diocese of Lima was geographically isolated and morally lax. Turibius made three visitations of the entire diocese (the first of these lasted seven years), staying several days in each community and enduring hardships without complaint. Turibius made a point of learning the Indians' languages; this helped him teach and minister to his people, and also made him a very successful missionary. As bishop, he denounced exploitation of the Indians by Spanish nobles and even clergy; he imposed many reforms, in spite of considerable opposition. Turibius organized a seminary in 1591 — the first in the Western hemisphere — and his pastoral example inspired reforms in other dioceses under Spanish administration. He was assisted by St. Francis Solanus and by his friend St. Rose of Lima, and served as Archbishop of Lima for twenty-six years, dying in 1606.

LESSONS

1. True holiness will often require a willingness to upset the status quo. When St. Turibius observed exploitation of the Indians and other abuses, he sided with them, not with his Spanish countrymen, and — in spite of opposition and resentment — insisted that they be treated fairly.

2. If we are to share the Gospel with others, we first need to have some willingness to understand and accept them as persons valuable in and of themselves. St. Turibius demonstrated this by learning the Indians' languages; we can show this respect for others by taking the time to listen to them (instead of coming across as all-knowing missionaries who have nothing to learn from others).

April

April 2 — St. Francis of Paola (Hermit)

St. Francis of Paola (1416–1507) was an Italian hermit
and the founder of a religious order. As a boy, he accompanied his parents on a pilgrimage to Rome and Assisi. Deeply
moved, he decided to spend his life in prayer and meditation. For a short time Francis was with the Franciscans, but
then went off to live as a hermit in a cave overlooking the
sea near the town of Paola. Before Francis turned twenty,
he was joined by other young men who wished to share
in the contemplative life. A religious order was formed,
and eventually approved by the Church in 1474; Francis
named it the "Minims" (from the Latin *minimi*, meaning
"the least"), and insisted his followers live a very austere
lifestyle, with much emphasis on prayer, meditation, and
fasting. He himself was blessed with many spiritual gifts,
such as the ability to perform miracles, to read minds, and
to prophesy; though an unlearned man, he moved others
by his wisdom and sincerity. Though he preferred a life
of prayer and solitude, Francis realized God was calling
him to be active in the world. He defended the poor and
oppressed, even to the point of admonishing the King of
Naples to give up his sins. King Louis XI of France heard
of Francis' reputation, and begged him to come and heal
him of a possibly fatal disease, promising him great rewards. Francis refused until ordered to go by the Pope;
when Louis begged him to cure him, he told the king to

pray to God alone. Francis didn't abandon the king, however; his wisdom and holiness helped prepare Louis for a holy death. During this time Francis used his influence in the royal court to promote peace between France and her neighbors, and after the king's death in 1483, he established his order in various French cities. St. Francis remained in France until his death in 1507.

LESSONS

1. One of the gifts for which we will be held accountable is our influence over others (even if we haven't sought or desired this); we must use this influence in a positive way, as St. Francis did with the young men who came to him, and with King Louis XI and the French royal court.

2. Great spiritual gifts (even those we might consider miraculous) are sometimes given to God's servants after much prayer and sacrifice, but these are only intended for God's glory and for serving others.

April 4 — St. Isidore of Seville (Bishop and Doctor)

The Spanish bishop and scholar St. Isidore of Seville (560?–636) was born in Cartagena; there were three other canonized saints in his family, including his older brother St. Leander. Leander, who was twenty years older than Isidore, was responsible for his education; because he was so strict, Isidore ran away. Sitting alone in the woods, he noticed a stone worn down by water, one drop at a time, and realized that he could satisfy his brother in the same way: by learning a little bit at a time. Isidore returned to his studies, and eventually became a great scholar. Leander became bishop of Seville; about the year 600, when Leander died, Isidore succeeded him, and remained as bishop of Seville for the rest of his life. He greatly strengthened the Church in Spain, establishing seminaries and religious houses, organizing church councils, and seeking to convert the Visigoths (a Germanic tribe which had invaded Spain) to Catholicism. Isidore continued his scholarly endeavors, authoring a dictionary, an encyclopedia, a history of the Goths, and a history of the world; during his last few months, he increased his charities so much that his house was filled with beggars from dawn to nightfall. St. Isidore died in 636, and was later declared a Doctor (an eminent and reliable teacher) of the Church.

LESSONS

1. Holy parents often have holy children. Severinus and Theodora were themselves very virtuous, and four of their children — Leander, Fulgentius, Florentina, and Isidore — became canonized saints.

2. Jesus' story about the powerless widow who finally received justice through her perseverance (Luke 18:1–7) is paralleled in the life of St. Isidore, who as a boy realized that great things could be accomplished simply by doing what he was capable of, a little bit at a time. We too are called to use our talents and to do our best, no matter how little or unimportant it seems, without giving up.

April 5 — St. Vincent Ferrer (Priest)

St. Vincent Ferrer (1350?–1419) was a Dominican priest caught up in the Great Western Schism — a period of almost forty years in which the Church was divided between two separate popes, each claiming to be the legitimate successor to St. Peter. Vincent was born in Spain; entering the Dominican Order, he developed a reputation as a brilliant scholar and powerful preacher. After being ordained a priest by Cardinal Peter de Luna, Vincent was chosen as prior of the monastery in Valencia. In 1378 an Italian cardinal was elected pope, taking the name Urban VI; however, his heavy-handed efforts at reform alienated some of the French cardinals, who declared his election invalid and chose as pope a different cardinal, who took the name Clement VII. This was very confusing for loyal Catholics; Vincent supported Clement, while St. Catherine of Siena backed Urban. (Most Church scholars today agree that Urban and his successors represented the legitimate line of the papacy.) Vincent tried to organize Spanish support for Clement; when Clement died, Vincent's mentor Cardinal de Luna was chosen to replace him, and took the name Benedict XIII. Vincent served as Benedict's confessor, and then spent ten years doing intensive mission work in France, Spain, and elsewhere, all the while promoting reconciliation and unity in the Church. Efforts were made to resolve the schism, including the election of a compromise pope with the idea of uniting the two factions (though this merely increased the number of claimants to the papal throne from two to three). Finally a general council was arranged in 1415, with the understanding that all three popes would resign and a new one be officially named.

This new pope chose the name Martin V — but Benedict XIII, in spite of Vincent's urgings, refused to resign as promised. Vincent finally concluded that Benedict wasn't the real pope, and publicly withdrew his support from him; this forced Benedict to flee, eventually ending the Great Schism. St. Vincent Ferrer continued preaching throughout Western Europe until his death in 1419.

LESSONS

1. Even saints can disagree (as St. Vincent did with St. Catherine) or be mistaken on important issues.

2. Persons having great influence or prestige must use these gifts for the well-being of the Church, as Vincent did by withdrawing his support from Benedict, even if it means admitting one was mistaken.

April 7 — St. John Baptist de La Salle (Priest and Founder)

St. John Baptist de La Salle (1651–1719) was a French priest who became famous as a teacher of underprivileged boys. John, who came from a noble family, was ordained a priest at twenty-seven, and was assigned to the city of Rheims, a very prestigious position. It seemed his life would be one of privilege and easy dignity, but as he became aware of the needs of poor children — especially education — he felt himself called to respond (even though at first the work was distasteful to him). John left Rheims and gave away his share of the family fortune. He began training a group of young men as teachers, thus beginning the order known today as the Christian Brothers. John successfully introduced several new educational methods (such as teaching in the local language, instead of Latin), and he established colleges for training teachers. His success in training delinquent and underprivileged boys provoked bitter opposition from secular schoolmasters, who resented his emphasis on Christian values; ignoring his critics, John urged his teachers to treat their students with love and compassion, making time for them and being concerned for their spiritual well-being. St. John Baptist de La Salle suffered from asthma and rheumatism in his last years; he died on Good Friday in 1719.

LESSONS

1. Our calling from God may at first be distasteful to us, but if we persevere, we will learn to love the life God intends for us. St. John Baptist de La Salle initially didn't want to work with children, but he obeyed the Lord's will, and ended up being very happy and fulfilled in his educational ministry.

2. As John learned, educating young people is an important way of serving Christ — especially by preparing them for eternity through an emphasis on faith and morality.

April 11 — St. Stanislaus (Bishop and Martyr)

The Polish bishop and martyr St. Stanislaus (1030–1079) was born near Krakow in Poland. After initial studies in Poland, he completed his education in Paris, where he spent seven years studying canon law and theology; this entitled him to a doctorate, but he refused it out of humility, and returned home. When his parents died, Stanislaus gave away his inheritance, and was ordained a priest. Stanislaus was appointed as preacher and archdeacon to the bishop of Krakow; his great eloquence and piety generated a spirit of renewal and conversion in the local community. When the bishop died in 1072, Stanislaus was unanimously elected as his successor; because of the importance of this position, he soon found himself involved in the political affairs of the Polish kingdom. Bishop Stanislaus was outspoken in his attacks upon political and social injustice, particularly that of the bellicose and immoral King Boleslaus II, who warred with his neighbors and oppressed the peasantry. The king at first made a show of repenting, but soon returned to his evil ways. Stanislaus continued to denounce him, accusations of treason and threats of death notwithstanding. In 1079 the bishop excommunicated Boleslaus. The enraged king ordered his soldiers to murder Stanislaus; when they refused, he killed the bishop with his own hands while Mass was being celebrated. Because of Stanislaus' popularity, King Boleslaus was forced to flee to Hungary, where he's said to have spent the rest of his life doing penance in a Benedictine monastery. St. Stanislaus is considered the patron of Poland.

LESSONS

1. A complete "separation of Church and State" isn't always possible, nor — from a Christian perspective — always desirable. As St. Stanislaus knew, Christians must use their influence to oppose injustice, even if this means becoming involved in politics.

2. Humility and generosity are "gentle" virtues, but they can help prepare us for fierce and difficult struggles. Stanislaus' humility (in refusing a doctorate) and generosity (in giving away his fortune) allowed God to fill him with the courage and strength needed to resist the king.

April 13 — St. Martin I (Pope and Martyr)

Little or nothing is known of the early life of the seventh century Pope and martyr St. Martin I. A member of the Roman clergy, he was elected Pope in 649, and immediately found himself in the center of a religious and political controversy. In the Byzantine (Eastern) Empire there was a heresy, or false teaching, known as *Monothelitism*, which said that Christ, while on earth, had no human will, but only a divine one. (The Church teaches that Jesus has two wills: a full and perfect divine one, and a full and perfect human one.) Several of the Eastern emperors had favored Monothelitism, supported by the patriarch, or bishop, of the imperial city of Constantinople. Soon after his election, Pope Martin convened a Church council in Rome which officially rejected this teaching and condemned the efforts of the patriarch and emperor to promote it. An angered emperor tried to discredit and later to assassinate the Pope. Failing in these efforts, the emperor sent troops to Rome with orders to arrest Martin. Already in poor health, Martin made no resistance, and in the imperial city he suffered torture and imprisonment. He later wrote, "For forty-seven days I have not been given water to wash in. I am frozen through and wasting away with dysentery. The food I get makes me ill. But God sees all things and I trust in Him." Pope Martin was exiled to Crimea, where he died in 655.

St. Martin I is honored as a martyr because of his death in exile; he was the last pope to suffer martyrdom.

LESSONS

1. Truth is sometimes "politically incorrect," but — as St. Martin knew — followers of Christ must defend the Faith nonetheless, even at the risk of controversy and personal suffering.

2. St. Martin suffered greatly at the hands of his enemies, but was sustained by his trust in God. We too must remember that God sees all things, including the difficulties and injustices we experience, and that remaining steadfast will result in vindication and glory.

April 21 — St. Anselm (Bishop and Doctor)

The English bishop and theologian St. Anselm (1033–1109) was one of the Church's greatest medieval thinkers. Anselm was born of a noble family. At the age of fifteen he desired to enter a monastery, but his father forbade this. Anselm thereupon abandoned religion for a number of years and adopted a carefree lifestyle. He later repented of this, however, and in 1059 he entered the monastery of Bec in the French province of Normandy. After three years Anselm was elected prior (an important position within the community), and fifteen years after that, the monks unanimously chose him as abbot. Anselm devoted himself to scholarship and prayer during his thirty-four years in the monastery. He was one of the leading figures in Scholastic theology, which attempted to uncover religious truths through rational arguments and propositions (indeed, he became known as the Father of Scholasticism). At the request of his community, he published his theological works, the best-known of which is *Why God Became Man*. Anselm is also known for a definition or "proof" of God ("God is that of which nothing greater can be conceived"). Anselm's life entered a new phase in 1093 when he was appointed Archbishop of Canterbury; from then on he was constantly defending the Church's rights against the English monarchs William II and Henry I. Though Anselm was personally a kind and gentle person (and also, by that time, in frail health), he uncompromisingly upheld the Church's position. His courage impressed many, but William had him exiled. Anselm went to Rome for three years, returning to England upon William's death. King Henry I, however, was also unfriendly to the Church, and Anselm ended up spending a further three years in exile. St. Anselm finally returned to England, and died at Canterbury in 1109; he was canonized in 1720 and declared a Doctor (an eminent and reliable teacher) of the Church.

LESSONS

1. Parents have a duty of encouraging their children's vocations; if they forbid a particular response to God, the children may abandon the faith entirely — and the parents will share the responsibility for this. Fortunately for Anselm's father, his son later heard and answered God's call.

2. Reason and logic, while not a substitute for faith, can help people become aware of God's existence.

3. There are many ways of serving God; sometimes the same person may be called to two very different vocations — in which the earlier helps prepare him or her for the later. St. Anselm's years of prayer and study helped "gird him for battle" in his defense of the Church's rights against the English kings.

April 23 — St. George (Martyr)

The martyr St. George is well-known because of the many popular legends about him; the historical facts about his life, however, are less well-known and much more prosaic than the myths suggest. George lived in the third or fourth century, and was probably martyred about 303 in the Palestinian city of Lydda. It was there that veneration of him as a soldier-saint began, though the Church initially recognized that it knew little about his actual life (as late as the sixth century he was referred to as merely a good man "whose deeds are known only to God"). Unreliable legends about St. George developed in the Middle Ages; he was supposedly a knight from Cappadocia whose rescue of a maiden from a dragon in Libya prompted a large number of conversions. Other stories about him are also without factual basis, but St. George is nonetheless considered a patron saint of England, Portugal, Germany, Aragon, Genoa, and Venice.

LESSONS

1. The legend of St. George fighting and overcoming the dragon (a traditional symbol of evil) reminds us of God's care: "Under the Lord's wings you shall take refuge;

His faithfulness is a buckler and shield. You shall not fear the terror of the night, nor the arrow that flies by day" (Psalm 91:4–5).

2. People — including Christians — have a natural need for heroes, and stories about the saints — even if based on uncertain legends, as in the case of St. George — are a legitimate response to this need.

April 24 — St. Fidelis of Sigmaringen (Priest and Martyr)

St. Fidelis (1577–1622) was born in the German town of Sigmaringen as Mark Rey. He became a lawyer as a young man, and dedicated himself to upholding the rights of the poor and oppressed; in fact, he was nicknamed "the poor man's lawyer." Mark became disgusted by the widespread corruption he observed. His brother George was a Franciscan friar of the Capuchin Order, and Mark decided to join the Order himself and to become a priest. He gave his wealth to the poor and entered the Capuchins, choosing the religious name Fidelis (Latin for "faithful"). Fidelis combined a life of continued service to the poor with an austere lifestyle, spending many hours in prayer, penance, and all-night vigils. Speaking of Fidelis, Pope Benedict XIV (d. 1758) once said: "With wealth collected from the powerful and from princes, he comforted widows and orphans in their loneliness. He was always helping prisoners in their spiritual and bodily needs. He showed constant zeal in visiting and comforting the sick whom he would win back to God and prepare for their last struggle. The most outstanding example of this meritorious way of life occurred when the Austrian army, stationed in the area of Raetia, was almost totally destroyed by an epidemic. To show compassion he used to bring food for the weak and the dying." Fidelis led a group of Capuchins to Switzerland, where they preached against the Calvinists and Zwinglians (followers of the Protestant leaders John Calvin and Ulrich Zwingli). Their mission was quite dangerous, but was very successful in bringing people back to the Church. Even though his life was threatened, Fidelis went to preach at the town of Seewis; while there, a gun was fired at him, but he escaped harm. A sympathetic Protestant offered him shelter, but Fidelis declined, stating that his life was in God's hands. Upon leaving town, he was attacked by a group of armed men and killed.

LESSONS

1. The Christian response to social problems isn't simply to complain about them, but to do something to help those who suffer. St. Fidelis tried to improve society — first as a lawyer, then as a priest.

2. Our Catholic faith is worth dying for; as St. Fidelis once wrote, "What is it that today makes true followers of Christ cast luxuries aside, leave pleasures behind, and endure difficulties and pain? It is living faith that expresses itself through love."

April 25 — St. Mark (Evangelist)

Most of our knowledge about St. Mark, author of one of the Four Gospels, comes directly from the New Testament. It is possible that the unnamed young man present at Jesus' arrest (Mark 14:51–52) was the evangelist himself; Mark is mentioned directly in several places in the Acts of the Apostles. He was the son of a Christian woman in Jerusalem named Mary; it was to her house that St. Peter fled following his miraculous escape from prison (12:12). Mark was a cousin of St. Barnabas, and he accompanied Barnabas and St. Paul on one of their missionary journeys. However, Mark turned back for some unknown reason (12:25; 13:13); this prompted an angry St. Paul to refuse to take him along on his next journey. Mark instead went with Barnabas to preach the Good News in Cyprus (15:37–39). Eventually Mark was reconciled with St. Paul, whom he visited when the latter was imprisoned in Rome. Mark probably wrote his Gospel while in Rome, perhaps around the year 60. An early tradition identifies Mark as the interpreter or secretary of St. Peter; the apostle's recollections may indeed have been one of the sources of the Gospel.

LESSONS

1. Jesus once said, "Whoever sets his hand to the plow but keeps looking back is unfit for the Kingdom" (Luke 9:62) — but the Lord also gives a second chance to those who fail. St. Mark abandoned Paul and Barnabas on their missionary journey, but later succeeded in his efforts to share the Good News.

2. Mark's Gospel is blunt in describing the weaknesses and failures of the apostles (and if the young man in 14:51–52 is the evangelist, he also includes something that was personally embarrassing); being a Christian requires a commitment to the truth — even when it is painful or disconcerting.

April 28 — St. Peter Chanel (Priest and Martyr)

The son of a French peasant, St. Peter Chanel (1803–1841) became a priest as a young man, and within three years brought about a spiritual renewal in his parish by showing great devotion to the sick. However, he desired to be a missionary, and at age twenty-eight joined the Society of Mary (the Marists). For five years Peter taught in the Marist seminary; then he and several other missionaries were sent to the New Hebrides Islands in the Pacific. Peter, a Marist brother, and an English layman were assigned to the island of Futuna, whose ruler Niuliki had only recently stamped out cannibalism. At first the missionaries were well-received, and Peter devoted himself to learning the local language and adjusting to life with whalers, traders, and warring native tribes. He remained gentle and calm in spite of great physical want and an apparent lack of success as a missionary. Eventually Peter won the confidence of many natives, and he began making converts. One of his catechumens said, "He loves us. He does what he teaches. He forgives his enemies. His teaching is good." However, Niuliki became increasingly suspicious, and when his own son converted to Catholicism, he reacted violently. In 1841, three years after his arrival on Futuna, St. Peter Chanel was seized by Niuliki's warriors and clubbed to death, becoming the first martyr of the South Seas.

LESSONS

1. Our Christian example is of vital importance in converting others or in bringing about a spiritual renewal; St. Peter Chanel's personal example testified to the truth of the Gospel he proclaimed.

2. As Niuliki's reaction shows, some people are threatened by the Gospel, and may react unfavorably or even violently, as Jesus foretold (Luke 21:12–17).

April 29 — St. Catherine of Siena (Virgin and Doctor)

St. Catherine of Siena (1347–1380) was the youngest of twenty-five children, and her parents hoped she would marry a wealthy young man — but she had already dedicated her life to God. When her mother nagged her about making herself attractive, Catherine, in a gesture of defiance, cut off her beautiful hair so no one would want to marry her. She was punished by being given the hardest work and forced to wait on all the other family members; Catherine's cheerful obedience led to her father's decreeing that she be left in peace. For some years Catherine lived as a recluse in her room, praying and meditating; then, at age eighteen, she entered the Dominican Order. Italy was touched by a plague, and Catherine spent much time caring for the poor and the sick. Her remarkable love and devotion attracted others, and gradually a group formed about her, including lay persons, priests, and religious. In 1375 Catherine gained an international reputation by mediating the conflict between the papacy and the city of Florence, and then used her influence to advise kings and make political treaties. Catherine was influential in convincing the timid Pope Gregory XI to leave Avignon in France (where the popes had resided for many years) and return to Rome, freeing the Church from excessive French influence. This success was short-lived, however, for in 1378 Gregory died, and the Great Schism — a division of allegiance between two separate popes — developed. Catherine steadfastly supported Pope Urban VI, the properly-elected successor to Gregory, but the schism was not resolved for almost forty years. In 1380 St. Catherine died at the age of only thirty-three, surrounded by her followers; much of Europe mourned her passing. She was known as a visionary and mystic, and some of her writings are still widely used; in 1970 Pope Paul VI declared her a Doctor (an eminent and reliable teacher) of the Church — one of the few women to be so honored.

LESSONS

1. Catherine was "stubborn" as a child in pursuing her vocation, but also cheerful and obedient — and it was these qualities which convinced her father to give in to her wishes. We too must be firm in our faith — but in a way that attracts others, rather than condemning or alienating them.

2. In an era in which women were in many ways oppressed, St. Catherine found true "liberation" — not by political movements or activism, but by surrendering completely to Christ.

April 30 — St. Pius V (Pope)

St. Pius V (1504–1572) was the Pope entrusted with en-
forcing the decrees and reforms of the Council of Trent.
Born in Italy as Michael Ghislieri, he came from a humble background, and as a youth entered the Dominican
Order. Michael developed a reputation as a preacher and
teacher; in 1556 he was appointed a bishop, and the following year, a cardinal. Cardinal Ghislieri strongly supported the reforms of the Church enacted by the Council
of Trent (1545–1563), and in 1566 he was elected Pope (with
the help of the reform-minded Cardinal St. Charles Borromeo). During his six-year reign, Pius ordered the establishment of seminaries for the training of priests, published
a new missal (which remained in use for 400 years), and set
up Confraternity of Christian Doctrine classes (CCD) for
the young. Pius sought, sometimes unsuccessfully, to uphold the Church's political authority against various European nations. Queen Elizabeth's interference with Church
affairs in England led to her excommunication by Pius;
the Pope also struggled against the ambitions of the Holy
Roman Emperor and King Philip II of Spain. Pius' greatest secular triumph was his sponsorship of the European
fleet which defeated the Turkish navy in the Battle of Lep-
anto in 1571, thus saving Europe from a Turkish invasion.
Pius was unswerving in his efforts to improve the Church;
many people criticized his methods, but he had the respect
of the Roman people, for he established hospitals to care
for the sick and distributed food to the poor. In his own
personal life Pius remained true to his Dominican origins;
unlike some of his predecessors, he lived very simply and
devoted much time to prayer.

LESSONS

1. Because of human sinfulness, the Church is always in need of reform — just as are individual Christians. St. Pius responded by implementing Trent's decrees and by promoting solid religious education.

2. Even saints acting in a just cause aren't guaranteed worldly or political success; some of Pius' efforts failed (as when his excommunication of Elizabeth I resulted in a persecution of English Catholics). However, in the words of Mother Teresa of Calcutta, "God calls us not to be successful, but to be faithful."

May

May 1 — St. Joseph the Worker

May 1, or "May Day," was celebrated throughout the Communist world as a way of supposedly honoring the role and importance of laborers in Marxist countries. The Communist conception of work as almost an end in itself was, of course, very different from the Christian understanding, and in 1955, to highlight this difference, Pope Pius XII instituted the feast of St. Joseph the Worker. Joseph, the husband of Mary and the foster-father of Jesus, spent a lifetime laboring as a carpenter. His primary motivation for working wasn't a quest for riches or status, but a desire to serve God and to care for his family in a loving way. Joseph never worked any miracles; he never made any important speeches; he wasn't a public figure, but was known only as a humble carpenter (Matthew 13:55). Joseph labored in obscurity, but was nonetheless given an important part in God's plan.

LESSONS

1. Work is not intended to be an end in itself or a path to earthly riches; rather, it's meant to glorify God and to help us prepare for eternity. As Jesus said, "Do not store up for yourselves treasures on earth, where moth and decay destroy, and thieves break in and steal. But store up treasures in Heaven, where neither moth nor decay destroys,

nor thieves break in and steal. For where your treasure is, there also will your heart be" (Matthew 6:20–21).

2. Honest and humble labor is a source of true human dignity. Though St. Joseph worked as a simple carpenter, he achieved great holiness, and his example influenced Jesus, Who — though the eternal Son of God and the Source of all creation — Himself learned from Joseph and for a time followed in his footsteps as a carpenter (Mark 6:3).

May 2 — St. Athanasius (Bishop and Doctor)

St. Athanasius (296?–373) was a great Egyptian bishop who played a major role in opposing the heresy of Arianism and in preserving the Church's true faith. He was born of a Christian family in Alexandria, where he received a classical education. In 319 Athanasius was ordained a deacon, and later became a priest; he served as secretary to Bishop Alexander, who vigorously opposed the Arian heresy. This false belief, named after Arius, a priest who promoted it, claimed that Jesus wasn't truly divine, but merely human. After being expelled from Alexandria, Arius gathered support elsewhere, and soon his heresy became widespread. In 325 Athanasius accompanied Bishop Alexander to the Council of Nicea, which officially condemned Arianism — but the Arian controversy had barely begun. Alexander died shortly after the Council, recommending on his deathbed that his secretary Athanasius be chosen as his successor. Athanasius ruled his diocese some forty-six years, struggling with Arianism throughout this period. Arius gained the sympathy of the emperor, and his heresy flourished; many bishops and priests abandoned the Church's true teaching, accepting Arianism instead. The emperor ordered Athanasius to reinstate the heretical priest; when the Bishop refused to do so, he was banished from Egypt. On four separate occasions Athanasius was sent into exile (spending seventeen of his forty-six years as bishop away from his diocese); nothing, however, could make him cease defending the divinity of Christ. St. Athanasius played perhaps the major role in helping the Church eventually overcome Arianism (though it continued for some years after his death in 373); for this reason, and because of his learned writings (including the *Life of St. Anthony*), he is considered a Doctor (an eminent and reliable teacher) of the Church.

LESSONS

1. As St. Athanasius realized, Christian truth is unchanging and worth defending, even at the cost of considerable personal sacrifice.

2. In his *Life of St. Anthony*, Athanasius described the great monk's many struggles with demons, while he himself spent his life fighting against the Church's enemies. St. Athanasius recognized the reality of evil and of human sinfulness — but he firmly believed in the all-conquering power of Christ.

May 3 — Saints Philip and James (Apostles)

St. James is listed in the Gospels as the son of Alphaeus; he was sometimes referred to as St. James "the Lesser," to distinguish him from St. James "the Greater," who was also an apostle and was the brother of St. John. James' brother

St. Jude was also an apostle, and their mother Mary was a close relative of the Blessed Virgin; for that reason, James was sometimes called the brother (cousin) of the Lord. Perhaps because of his relationship to Jesus, James had an important role in the early Church, being considered the first bishop of Jerusalem; he was martyred about the year 62. St. Philip came from Bethsaida in Galilee, which was also the hometown of Peter and his brother Andrew. After being called as an apostle by Jesus, Philip in turn sought out Nathanael, describing Jesus as "the One of Whom Moses spoke" (John 1:43–49). At the Last Supper it was Philip who asked Jesus to show them the Father (John 14:8–9); he, like the other disciples, was slow to realize the union between God the Father and the Christ. According to an early Church legend, Philip preached the Gospel in Phrygia (in modern-day Turkey), where he may have suffered martyrdom.

LESSONS

1. When someone praised Mary for her maternal relationship to Jesus, He responded, "Rather, blessed are those who hear the word of God and keep it" (Luke 11:28). St. James' holiness came not from being related to Jesus in a biological way, but in a spiritual one — and this is a relationship Our Lord offers to every one of His followers.

2. Upon meeting Jesus, St. Philip's first impulse was to share the news with his friend Nathanael. Philip's example reminds us that, as *good news*, the Gospel is meant to be shared with others; every Christian is called to evangelize in one way or another.

May 12 — Saints Nereus and Achilleus (Martyrs)

The first century martyrs Saints Nereus and Achilleus were Roman soldiers and members of the elite Praetorian Guard, entrusted with the responsibility of defending the Roman Emperor. Upon converting to Christianity, they were arrested, taken to the island of Terracina, and martyred. Aside from this, nothing else is known about them. Three centuries later, Pope St. Damasus (d. 384) wrote of them: "The martyrs Nereus and Achilleus had enrolled themselves in the army and exercised the cruel office of carrying out the orders of the tyrant [the Emperor], being ever ready, through the constraint of fear, to obey his will. O miracle of faith! Suddenly they cease from their fury, they become converted, they fly from the camp of their wicked leader; they throw away their shields, their armor and their blood-stained javelins. Confessing the faith of Christ, they rejoice to bear testimony to its triumph. Learn now from the words of Damasus what great things the glory of Christ can accomplish." According to St. Damasus, the two martyrs were buried in the cemetery of Domitilla on the Via Ardeatina near Rome.

LESSONS

1. Saints Nereus and Achilleus were not the first enemies or persecutors of the Church to undergo a dramatic conversion and then join the group they had been persecuting; Saul of Tarsus, who vigorously opposed the early Christians, shocked many people (including the Christians themselves) by becoming not only a Christian, but the Church's greatest missionary. Unexpected conversions such as these

are a vivid reminder of the power of the Gospel and of divine grace. No matter how bleak a situation may appear, God is able to bring about amazing changes in fortune, validating Jesus' promise that the gates of hell shall not prevail against the Church (cf. Matthew 16:18).

2. Pope St. Gregory the Great (d. 604) said on the feast of Nereus and Achilleus, "These saints, before whom we are assembled, despised the world and trampled it under their feet when peace, riches and health gave it charms." Like them, we are called to seek God's Kingdom first, and not the wealth and success this world offers (cf. Luke 12:31–34).

May 12 — St. Pancras (Martyr)

In addition to being the feast day of Saints Nereus and Achilleus, May 12 is also the feast of St. Pancras, another martyr about whom very little is known. According to legend, Pancras (also known as Pancratius) lived at the end of the third century and belonged to a noble family in Phrygia (a region in modern-day Turkey); he became a Christian while a boy, and was baptized at age fourteen. When Pancras gave away all his possessions to the poor, this attracted the attention of the authorities, and he was discovered to be a Christian. He refused to renounce his faith, and was beheaded about 304 during the persecution decreed by the Emperor Diocletian. St. Pancras was buried in a cemetery which was later named after him. When St. Augustine of Canterbury came to England several centuries later, he named the first church built there after St. Pancras; this ancient church eventually gave its name to the famous St. Pancras Railway Station in modern-day London.

LESSONS

1. Living out our faith can attract unfavorable attention; St. Pancras' lavish generosity directly resulted in his discovery and execution. There may be times when secrecy and prudence are called for, but — as St. Pancras knew — as Christians we must let our light shine before all (cf. Matthew 5:16), in spite of the risks involved.

2. Young people are quite capable of making a true commitment to Christ; even though he was only fourteen when martyred, St. Pancras managed to achieve the fullness of life in Christ.

3. Jesus had warned His followers of the possibility of persecution (Luke 21:12–15), but — as St. Pancras discovered — He fulfills His promise to sustain those who suffer in His Name.

May 14 — St. Matthias (Apostle)

All our knowledge of St. Matthias comes from the Acts of the Apostles, which describes his election as an apostle (1:15–26). Because of Judas' betrayal of Jesus and subsequent suicide, Our Lord's original and closest followers — the Apostles — numbered eleven, rather than twelve (though by this time there were many other followers of Christ, and their numbers were constantly growing). Since the Apostles held the role of elders or leaders in the early Church, St. Peter suggested that a replacement for Judas be selected from among those who had known Jesus during His earthly ministry. Two such disciples were nominated: Joseph (known as Barsabbas) and Matthias. After praying

over them, the Apostles chose by lot — and Matthias was
thus selected. From that time on he was numbered among
the Twelve Apostles. Apart from this description in Acts,
St. Matthias is nowhere else mentioned in the New Testament. However, an ancient tradition plausibly claims that
Matthias was one of Jesus' seventy-two disciples, and another tradition states that he suffered martyrdom in Asia
Minor (modern-day Turkey), along the shore of the Black
Sea.

LESSONS

1. Sometimes we may feel we don't "fit in," especially
when it comes to taking on important responsibilities or
working with influential people in the Church or in society.
However, if God is calling us to such a role, He will also
make it possible for us to achieve it. St. Matthias, though
too humble to consider himself equal to the other apostles,
was nonetheless able to exercise this office.

2. The Church has the authority to make binding decisions in response to particular issues or questions that may
arise. Jesus is nowhere recorded as having told the Apostles
to replace Judas; St. Peter and the others themselves decided that this should be done, and the Holy Spirit ratified
this decision.

May 15 — St. Isidore the Farmer

St. Isidore the Farmer (1070–1130) is considered the patron saint of farmers and rural communities. (He is not to
be confused with another Spanish saint, St. Isidore of Seville
[April 4]). Isidore was born in Madrid; as a young boy, he

went to work on the estate of John de Vergas, a wealthy landowner from the nearby town of Torrelaguanna. Isidore labored on John's farm for the remainder of his life. He was a model worker, a simple and caring person, and a very devout Christian. Every day he rose early in the morning to attend Mass at a nearby church — sometimes, according to fellow workers, showing up late for work because he spent too much time in prayer. Isidore married Maria de la Cabeza, a simple and devout woman who herself became a canonized saint. The couple had one child, who died at an early age. They were both known for their piety and concern for the poor; legends exist about Isidore miraculously supplying them with food on occasion, and the saint had a great concern that animals be treated properly. Isidore would pray while plowing in the fields, and it's even said that angels would sometimes help him with his work. St. Isidore the Farmer died in 1130; along with Saints Ignatius of Loyola, Francis Xavier, Teresa of Avila, and Philip Neri, he is known in Spain as one of the "Five Saints."

LESSONS

1. Many Americans have a desire to build a successful career, changing jobs when better opportunities arise and perhaps even starting their own businesses and becoming their own bosses. God's grace can be experienced in such a lifestyle, but this measure of success is not required for holiness. St. Isidore worked for the same landowner for over fifty years; he had no need to become independent, for he realized that he was ultimately working for Christ.

2. Work and prayer can be and are meant to be combined. This might mean, if circumstances allow, arrang-

ing our schedule so as to attend daily Mass before or after work; it also quite frequently means praying or meditating while working (especially in the case of manual labor). St. Isidore worshipped God in both these manners, thereby sanctifying his work and influencing those around him.

May 18 — St. John I (Pope and Martyr)

St. John I was a sixth century pope and martyr. John was born in the Italian province of Tuscany, and was elected Bishop of Rome (that is, Pope) in 523. The Mediterranean world was, by this time, divided into the Eastern and Western Empires, each having a separate emperor. Christianity was also divided (though not in a geographic sense) by the Arian heresy, which denied the divinity of Christ. King Theodoric, the German chieftain who was in effect the Western emperor, was himself an Arian, though he was initially tolerant of the Catholics in his kingdom. Soon after John was elected Pope, Justin, the Eastern emperor, began repressing the Arians in the East. Theodoric was upset by this, and he forced John and other religious leaders from the West to visit Justin in Constantinople (capital of the Eastern empire) for the purpose of lessening the restrictions placed upon the Arians. (Because religious questions had political implications, it was not uncommon for kings to involve themselves in religion, and for bishops to find themselves involved in politics.) Little is known about the outcome of the negotiations Pope John conducted with Emperor Justin, but because the two leaders got along well together, a paranoid Theodoric assumed they were plotting against him. When John returned to Italy in 526, Theodoric had him arrested. Pope John died soon after he was imprisoned, perhaps as a result of the treatment he received, thus earning a martyr's crown. John was the first of twenty-three popes of that name, and the only one to be canonized a saint.

LESSON

Sometimes religion is inescapably involved in politics. As St. John knew, when this happens, our primary loyalty must be to Christ, not to the rulers of this world.

May 20 — St. Bernardine of Siena (Priest)

The Italian priest St. Bernardine of Siena (1380–1444) was known for his preaching and his popularity with ordinary people. As a young man, he cared for an elderly woman on her deathbed; she constantly pronounced the name "Jesus" with great devotion. Bernardine was profoundly affected, and decided to make the name of Jesus the theme of his own life. When Siena was struck by a plague, Bernardine nursed the sick until he himself became ill. After recovering, he became a Franciscan monk, and was ordained a priest in 1404. Bernardine spent a dozen years in solitude and prayer, and was then sent forth as a preacher. For many years he traveled on foot throughout Italy, preaching to crowds as large as 30,000 — accomplishing all this with a weak and hoarse voice (though, according to legend, it later miraculously improved because of his devotion to Mary). Bernardine was especially known for his devotion to the Holy Name of Jesus, and he devised a symbol — IHS (the first three letters of the name Jesus in Greek) — to represent it. As this devotion spread, the symbol began to replace the superstitious signs and symbols of the day. When a manufacturer of playing cards complained that the saint's preaching against gambling was depriving him of his livelihood, Bernardine told him to start making medallions with the symbol IHS. The man took this advice — and ended up making more money than ever. Some of Bernardine's teachings were criticized, and three attempts were made to have the pope discipline him, but the saint's obvious faith and holiness overcame all opposition. St. Bernardine helped strengthen the Franciscan Order, and he contributed to a great increase of piety among the laity. He died soon after attending the Council of Florence in 1444, and was canonized only six years later.

LESSONS

1. As St. Paul stated, "God bestowed upon Jesus the Name that is above every other name" (Philippians 2:9). As St. Bernardine realized, honoring the Holy Name of Jesus is the sign of a true Christian.

2. God will provide for those who, even at financial cost to themselves, seek to do what's right; St. Bernardine helped the maker of gambling equipment find a better and holier way to make a living.

3. Bernardine followed the advice of St. Francis of Assisi to preach about "vice and virtue, punishment and glory"; his success shows that many people are willing to listen to the proclamation of the truth.

May 25 — St. Bede the Venerable
(Monk and Doctor)

St. Bede (672?–735) was a British scholar and monk widely acknowledged as a saint even in his own lifetime. As a youth he was sent to the monastery of St. Paul in Jarrow, and it was there that he remained for virtually the remainder of his life. Bede became a monk and a priest, and the monastery provided the ideal setting for his great spiritual growth. It also provided the opportunity for him to write and study; he once said, "I have devoted my energies to the study of the Scriptures, observing monastic discipline, and singing the daily services in the Church; study, teaching, and writing have always been my delight." Bede was an expert in many fields of learning, including natural philosophy, astronomy, arithmetic, grammar, Church history, and Scripture; he authored many books, including the famous *History of the English Church and People*, and was the first known writer of English prose. As his reputation spread, various kings and even the pope desired his presence as a scholar-in-residence, but except for a few months teaching in the school of the Archbishop of York, Bede remained in the monastery of St. Paul until his death. Only a century after this St. Bede was unofficially given the title "Venerable" (worthy of honor), and in 1899 Pope Leo XIII declared him a Doctor (an eminent and reliable teacher) of the Church.

LESSONS

1. As the life of St. Bede shows, scholarship can lead to holiness; the Book of Wisdom states, "Resplendent and

unfading is Wisdom, and she is readily perceived by those who love her, and found by those who seek her" (6:12).

2. Serving God is more important than one's own reputation; rather than seeking honor as a scholar-in-residence, St. Bede preferred to continue his studying and writing in the obscurity of the monastery.

May 25 — St. Gregory VII (Pope)

One of the most important popes in the Church's history was St. Gregory VII (1020–1085). At that time the Church faced three major problems: *simony* (the buying and selling of sacred offices), the unlawful marriage of clergy (many priests ignored their vow of celibacy), and *lay investiture* (the practice of kings and nobles controlling the choice of Church officials). These problems had been growing worse for some time, but in 1049 the newly-elected Pope Leo IX resolved to reform the Church. To assist him, he brought to Rome a young monk named Hildebrand (Gregory's family name); though he desired a monastic life, Hildebrand recognized the importance of Leo's undertaking, and assisted him vigorously. Gregory himself was elected Pope in 1073; he followed through on Leo's reforms, and worked to strengthen the Church. He encountered much opposition, especially when he forbade the practice of lay investiture. This brought him into direct conflict with Emperor Henry IV of Germany. When Henry resorted to force, Gregory excommunicated him; Henry pretended to repent, and the excommunication was lifted; then the Emperor continued his opposition to the Pope. In 1084 Henry's troops captured Rome. A Catholic prince from Normandy recaptured the city for Gregory, but the loss of life and property was so great that the furious Romans forced the Pope to flee. Gregory went to Salerno, where he died in exile the following year. On his deathbed St. Gregory said, "I have loved righteousness and hated iniquity; that is why I die in exile."

LESSONS

1. Sometimes God uses our failures to further the advance of His Kingdom. Measured in worldly terms, St. Gregory failed in his confrontation with the emperor — but his courage and integrity helped spur the ongoing reform of the Church.

2. When it comes to serving God, our personal preference may not always coincide with His will. The young monk Hildebrand would have preferred a monastic life — but he freely gave up this vocation when he realized God was calling him to the more important mission of assisting Pope Leo's efforts at reform.

May 25 — St. Mary Magdalene de Pazzi (Virgin and Mystic)

Catherine de Pazzi (1566–1607) was born of a noble family in the Italian city of Florence during its golden age; instead of taking her expected role in society as a matron and mother, she chose to devote herself to meditation and the service of God. Catherine learned to meditate at the age of 9, and received her First Communion the following year (which was much earlier than normal at that time); soon afterward she made a vow of perpetual virginity. At the age of sixteen Catherine entered a Carmelite convent, choosing the name Mary Magdalene. One year later she became seriously ill. Because death seemed imminent, her superiors allowed her to make her final profession of vows. She was carried on a cot to the chapel for the ceremony, after which she experienced an ecstasy lasting two hours. This spiritual event was repeated each morning after Communion for the next forty days. Mary Magdalene's mystical experiences gave her great insight into the ways of God. At the request of her confessor, five volumes were dictated by her to other sisters describing the nature of her experiences and visions. All who came into contact with her were impressed by her faith and holiness, and it was said she had the gifts of bilocation (being in two different places at once) and reading minds. Mary Magdalene's special gifts were given her by God to prepare her for a five-year period of profound spiritual anguish and isolation, during which she had violent temptations and great physical suffering. She remained faithful to God through all this, and died peacefully at the age of forty-one.

LESSONS

1. Visions and mystical experiences are not necessary for holiness, but sometimes God grants these gifts to certain persons, such as St. Mary Magdalene de Pazzi, as a reminder of the new life awaiting us.

2. Saints are not immune to periods of dryness or aridity; as Mary Magdalene de Pazzi discovered, remaining faithful in spite of these experiences can be a source of great spiritual growth.

May 26 — St. Philip Neri (Priest and Founder)

The Italian priest St. Philip Neri (1515–1595) greatly contributed to the spiritual reformation of the Church in the sixteenth century. He was born in Florence to a wealthy family, and after receiving a good education, was apprenticed to a relative with a flourishing business — which Philip was intended to inherit. However, after having a mystical experience, Philip decided to devote himself entirely to religious matters. He went to Rome to study philosophy and theology, and supported himself by tutoring. Saddened by the immoral state of the city, Philip formed a group of young men who met regularly for prayer, study, and recreation. This "oratory" (named after the upper room where they met) was unique in combining a quest for virtue with laughter and an enjoyment of life. In 1551 Philip, at the urging of his confessor, was ordained a priest. He soon made a name for himself as a confessor, for he had the gift of reading hearts, and was gentle and friendly with penitents. Philip continued his work with young men, several of whom were ordained priests; with their help, he established an order called the Congregation of the Oratory. There was some opposition to the Oratory, for people were suspicious of a group in which laymen were actively involved, and in which the members enjoyed themselves while serving God and His people; nonetheless, Philip and his followers continued to influence many people through their example. Because of the great spiritual renewal that resulted from his efforts, St. Philip Neri was called "the Apostle of the city of Rome." He died in 1595, and was canonized in 1622.

LESSONS

1. Religion doesn't have to be a somber and unpleasant experience; as St. Philip Neri realized, faith and virtue can be combined with humor and a wholesome enjoyment of life — for life is meant to be a gift from God, not a burden to be endured.

2. St. Philip showed that holiness is both possible and practical; he emphasized that all Catholics — not only priests and religious — have a role to play in the life of the Church, for one of the ways we glorify God while also growing in grace is by using the gifts He has given us.

May 27 — St. Augustine of Canterbury (Bishop and Missionary)

The sixth century bishop St. Augustine of Canterbury (d. 605) is famous for his missionary work in England. (He is not to be confused with St. Augustine of Hippo, the great Church thinker of the fourth century). Augustine was the prior or abbot of a monastery in Rome. In 596 the Pope, St. Gregory the Great, chose him to lead a group of thirty monks on a missionary journey to England. (There were some scattered Christian communities there, but the land as a whole was still predominantly Anglo-Saxon and pagan.) Augustine's group set out, but on reaching France, heard terrifying stories of the treacherous waters of the English Channel and the ferocious temperament of the Anglo-Saxons. Augustine hurried back to confer with the Pope, but Gregory reassured him that his fears were groundless, and sent him back on his way. The missionaries arrived in England in 597; King Ethelbert, a pagan married to a Christian, received them kindly, and their work flourished. On Pentecost Sunday the king was baptized, along with many of his subjects. Augustine journeyed briefly to France, where he was consecrated a bishop, and then returned to England, establishing his see or diocese in Canterbury. The see at Canterbury continued to prosper, and additional dioceses were later established at London and Rochester. Not all of Augustine's efforts were successful; his attempts to reconcile the Anglo-Saxon converts and the original Christian inhabitants of England failed, and for a time the missionaries' work progressed slowly. By the time of St. Augustine's death in 605, however, a solid foundation for England's later widespread conversion to Christianity had been established.

LESSONS

1. Even saints can be reluctant to fulfill their mission; St. Augustine had to be encouraged by the Pope, who helped him overcome his fears by telling him, "He who would climb to a lofty height must go by steps, not leaps."

2. God is able to use us in spite of our weaknesses and failures, as long as we're willing to let His grace work in and through us.

June

June 1 — St. Justin (Martyr)

St. Justin (100?–165) was the first Christian philosopher. He was born of a pagan Greek family in Palestine (the Holy Land); as a young man, he studied one system of philosophy after another. He was principally attracted to Platonism (based on the teachings of Socrates and Plato some 500 years earlier), but through Platonism he came to know of and accept Christianity, finding that it answered great questions about life and existence better than the teachings of any earlier philosophers. Justin was about 33 when he became a Christian. He remained a layperson, but actively proclaimed the Gospel. He was an *apologist*, or defender of Christianity, and his writings (the *Apologies* and the *Dialogue with Trypho*) are valuable to us today because of the information they give about early Christian teachings and customs). Justin was a dedicated philosopher, combining Christianity with the best elements of Greek philosophical thought. He traveled widely as a missionary, twice staying in Rome. In the year 165 Justin was denounced as a Christian and arrested, along with five other men and a woman. Upon being ordered by the Roman prefect to offer sacrifice to the Roman gods, Justin replied, "No right-minded man forsakes truth for falsehood," and his companions said, "Do with us as you will — we are Christians, and we cannot sacrifice to idols." St. Justin and the others were thereupon beheaded; ever since then, he has been known as St. Justin the Martyr.

LESSONS

1. Sometimes an inadequate but sincere search for wisdom can lead a person to accept the truth of the Gospel; St. Justin's familiarity with Greek philosophy predisposed him to believe the claims of Christianity.

2. St. Justin realized that once we have discovered the truth, we must not forsake it for anything, even at the cost of our lives — for as Jesus said, "the truth will set you free" (John 8:32).

June 2 — Saints Marcellinus (Priest and Martyr) and Peter (Exorcist and Martyr)

Saints Marcellinus and Peter were Roman Christians who suffered martyrdom for their faith at the beginning of the fourth century. Marcellinus was a priest in Rome, and Peter was an exorcist. (At one point in the Church's history, exorcists comprised a minor order in the ecclesiastical hierarchy, ranking below deacons and sub-deacons). During the intense persecution of the Church ordered by the Emperor Diocletian, both men were arrested and imprisoned. According to legend, Marcellinus and Peter not only strengthened the faith of other Christians imprisoned with them; they also made new converts, including the jailer — a man named Arthemius — and his wife and daughter. Along with the other Christians, Marcellinus and Peter were condemned to death about the year 304; the two saints were taken to a wood outside Rome named Silva Nigra, where they were beheaded in secret (so that their place of burial wouldn't be known to the Church, and in the hopes

that their example of courage and faith would be forgotten). Ironically, their names have been preserved and venerated over the centuries in the Roman Canon (Eucharistic
Prayer I) used at Mass. Pope St. Damasus (d. 384) had,
while a boy, talked to Arthemius about the two saints; as
Pope, he later wrote an epitaph for their tombs.

LESSONS

1. As Jesus said, "Nothing is concealed that will not be
revealed, nor secret that will not be made known" (Matthew
10:26). The Roman authorities attempted to execute Saints
Marcellinus and Peter in secret so as to erase their memory — but through their courageous martyrdom, God has
granted them eternal renown.

2. Difficulties and misfortunes can actually provide opportunities for spreading the Gospel; Marcellinus and Peter
used their imprisonment as a way of bringing still more
people to know and follow Christ.

June 3 — St. Charles Lwanga and Companions (Martyrs)

The nineteenth century martyrs of Uganda were the
first black Catholic martyrs of Africa. St. Charles Lwanga
first learned of Christ from two members of the court of
an African chief named Mawulungungu. Charles became
a catechumen (one actively preparing for baptism); soon
after this, he entered the royal court of King Mwanga of
Uganda, where he served as an assistant to Joseph Mukaso,
head of the royal pages (errand boys). King Mwanga at first

favored Charles and the other pages (young men aged thirteen to thirty), but when they rejected his homosexual advances, the king grew angry, and ordered a persecution of "all those who pray" — meaning all Catholics. Joseph Mukaso, who had encouraged the pages to resist, was put to death at the king's command. On the night of Mukaso's execution, Charles requested and received baptism; then, following his friend's example, he attempted to protect the others from the king's demands. Charles and his companions were imprisoned. On June 3, 1886 he and some of the other Catholics were burned alive, while still others were killed by the sword. The remaining Ugandan martyrs were killed early in 1887. St. Charles Lwanga and his twenty-one companions were canonized by Pope Paul VI in 1964.

LESSONS

1. Contrary to what some of the Church's critics claim, Christianity is not merely a white, European institution; the Gospel is intended for persons of every language, nationality, and race, and all people are capable of receiving it and of following Christ faithfully and heroically.

2. God gives wisdom and strength to all who seek these gifts. St. Charles Lwanga, though young and still only a catechumen, was able to recognize immorality and able to refuse to take part in it.

3. Though homosexuality is considered "politically correct" in our society, homosexual acts are sinful — and committed Christians accept this truth and, with God's help, if necessary, avoid such activity.

June 5 — St. Boniface (Bishop and Martyr)

The missionary bishop and martyr St. Boniface (672?–754) has been called the "Apostle to the Germans." He was born in England and given the name Wynfrith, which he later changed to Boniface. Until about the age of forty, he was a Benedictine monk, devoted primarily to scholarship; then, in 718, Boniface permanently left England and went to Germany as a missionary. Christianity had earlier been established among the tribes of Germany, but, largely through the weakness and ignorance of the clergy, it had become riddled with superstition, and was affected by paganism and heresy. Boniface described these conditions on a journey to Rome in 722, and Pope Gregory II thereupon appointed him an archbishop and charged him with reforming and reinvigorating the German church. Boniface worked tirelessly among the Germans, preaching to the pagans and encouraging the Christians, and his efforts met with great success. He made a point of restoring the obedience of clergy to their bishops, thereby strengthening the larger principle of unity with Rome; he also stressed the universal nature of the Church by seeking financial support from his friends in England and by involving foreign missionaries in his work. Additionally, Boniface aided the Frankish kings in their reform of the Church in France, and did much to promote the unity of the Church in France and Germany with Rome. Though in his seventies, Boniface desired to convert the fierce pagans of Frisia (located in modern-day Holland). He and fifty-three companions went to Frisia for this purpose, but were ambushed and killed by the natives upon their arrival; St. Boniface himself is said to have been stabbed while reading in his tent.

LESSONS

1. "Old age" isn't necessarily a hindrance to doing valuable work for God's Kingdom. St. Boniface didn't begin his career as a missionary until age forty, and even in his seventies, he chose not to "retire," but to undertake a difficult and dangerous missionary journey.

2. The true Church is one, holy, catholic, and apostolic. St. Boniface particularly emphasized the first of these marks of the Church by emphasizing the importance of obedience and unity with Rome.

June 6 — St. Norbert (Bishop)

St. Norbert (1080?–1134) was born of a noble Rhineland family, and until about age thirty-five led the life of a courtier at various princely courts. Then, following a narrow escape from death, he underwent a conversion and dedicated his life to God. Norbert was ordained a priest, but his new enthusiasm antagonized many of the local clergy. Their opposition prompted him to sell all his goods and give the proceeds to the poor; he then went to visit the Pope. Pope Gelasius II gave Norbert permission to travel and preach wherever he wished. Norbert went to northern France, and was very effective in rekindling the faith of lukewarm Catholics. He and a young priest, Hugh of Fosses, established a religious order known as the Premonstratensian Canons, dedicated to the correction of heresies and to fostering a greater respect for the Blessed Sacrament. Norbert continued his itinerant preaching until 1126, when he was chosen as archbishop of Magdeburg in Germany. The diocese was badly in need of reform, and Norbert undertook his duties with customary enthusiasm. He reformed local abuses, renewed sacramental life in the diocese, and reconciled enemies — though he made enemies himself by trying to recover territory stolen from the Church (and this led to several attempts on his life). In 1130 Norbert supported Pope Innocent II in his struggle against an antipope, and just before his death was appointed chancellor for Italy. St. Norbert had a great devotion to the Holy Eucharist (his emblem is a monstrance, or "display case" for the Host); he died in 1134.

LESSONS

1. A close call with death is often an invitation from God to change one's life; St. Norbert realized this, and allowed his narrow escape to set him on the path to holiness.

2. As St. Norbert recognized, the Holy Eucharist is a great spiritual treasure, and deserves our profound gratitude and respect.

June 9 — St. Ephrem (Deacon and Doctor)

St. Ephrem (306?–373) was a Syrian poet and theologian. He was born in the Mesopotamian city of Nisibis; because of his Christian sympathies, his pagan father forced him to leave home. Ephrem was baptized a Christian, and became famous as a teacher. In 363 the Christian emperor was forced to cede Nisibis to the Persians. Ephrem, along with many other Christians, thereupon migrated to Edessa (in modern-day Iraq), where he soon gained a reputation for scholarship, especially in the Scriptures. Ephrem was ordained a deacon, though he later declined to be ordained to the priesthood. (According to one legend, he was also nominated as a bishop later in life. Feeling himself unworthy of this honor, he avoided it by feigning madness.) The Church in the fourth century was divided by many heresies and controversies. Ephrem opposed false teachings and forcefully upheld true Catholic doctrine. His unique and effective approach involved writing hymns against the heretics of the day; he would take popular songs of such groups and, using their melodies, compose very beautiful hymns expressing true doctrine. Ephrem was one of the first to introduce sung music into Christian worship, thereby continuing a venerable Old Testament and New Testament tradition (and gaining a reputation as "The Lyre of the Holy Spirit"). Ephrem also composed many other religious works, and after his death his writings were translated into Greek, Latin, and Armenian. In spite of his great fame, he maintained a simple and unpretentious lifestyle, living in a small cave outside Edessa. He died in 373, and in 1920 was declared a Doctor (an eminent and reliable teacher) of the Church.

LESSONS

1. Jesus once said, "Whoever loves father or mother more than Me is not worthy of Me" (Matthew 10:37). St. Ephrem was willing to give up his earthly family in order to belong to the family of God.

2. It's been said that "whoever sings, prays twice." Music and singing are powerful ways of expressing emotions

— and Ephrem realized they can be a valuable form of worship and of proclaiming the truth.

June 11 — St. Barnabas (Apostle)

Though not one of the Twelve Apostles, St. Barnabas, along with St. Paul, was considered an apostle and an important leader in the early Church. The Acts of the Apostles introduces him by saying, "There was a certain Levite from Cyprus named Joseph, to whom the apostles gave the name 'Barnabas' (meaning 'son of encouragement'). He sold a farm that he owned and made a donation of the money, laying it at the apostles' feet" (4:36–37). It was Barnabas who introduced Paul to Peter and the other apostles; his acceptance of this former persecutor of Christianity helped the other Christians overcome their distrust of Paul. When the Church in Jerusalem sent Barnabas as an official representative to the newly-formed Christian community in Antioch, he had Paul accompany him. The two men instructed the Christians there for a year. Recognizing Paul and Barnabas as inspired leaders, the church in Antioch sent the two to preach to the Gentiles (non-Jews). At Barnabas' insistence, they were accompanied by his cousin Mark (the eventual author of the Gospel) — but the young man deserted them when the journey proved to be hazardous. Paul and Barnabas traveled to Cyprus (Barnabas is regarded as the founder of the Church there) and throughout Greece; they had much success, though they also encountered opposition and persecution. When Paul refused to allow Mark to accompany them on a later missionary journey, Barnabas separated from Paul and took Mark with him to Cyprus; eventually all of them were reconciled. Little else is known about St. Barnabas, though one account states that he was martyred at the Cypriot port of Salamis.

LESSONS

1. Encouraging other Christians in their faith is an important ministry; St. Barnabas — a true "son of encouragement" — provides a noble example of this truth.

2. Even Christians constantly need to be reconciled to one another. Barnabas and Paul split up over Mark's earlier desertion, but all were eventually reunited in peace.

June 13 — St. Anthony of Padua (Priest and Doctor)

St. Anthony of Padua (1195–1231) was a Portuguese priest famous for his gifted preaching. He originally planned to join the Augustinian Order, but when he saw the bodies of the first Franciscans to be martyred for their faith, he was filled with an intense desire to become a missionary — and, he hoped, a martyr — himself. After joining the Franciscans, he preached to the Moslems of North Africa for a time, but a serious illness forced his return to Europe. Anthony attended an ordination at a monastery; through an oversight, no one had been assigned to preach. When it was hurriedly suggested that Anthony do so, he humbly but hesitantly obeyed — with amazing results. Anthony's years of prayer, study of Scripture, and poverty allowed God's Spirit to speak through him in a very powerful way. His unprepared sermon was a sensation, and for the remaining nine years of his life, Anthony traveled about preaching, correcting errors, and upholding the Church's true teachings. His words had an impact on both the learned and the simple, and helped many return to the faith. A great Scripture scholar and theologian, Anthony was the first Franciscan to teach theology to the other friars. He died while still young, and was buried at Padua. St. Anthony was canonized the year after his death in 1231, and was later declared a Doctor (an eminent and reliable teacher) of the Church.

LESSONS

1. God does not promise to fulfill all our desires, even our noble ones; St. Anthony's vocation involved neither missionary work nor martyrdom, for God had something different in mind for him.

2. Anthony, who is revered as a help in finding lost objects, discovered his own vocation of preaching by accident; things have a way of "turning up" for those who make a point of trusting in God.

3. It may take time to discover our true vocations; as St. Anthony wrote, "In His providence Christ conceals the saints in a hidden place that they may not shine before others when they might wish to do so. Yet they are always ready to exchange the quiet of contemplation for the works of mercy as soon as they perceive in their heart the invitation of Christ."

June 19 — St. Romuald (Abbot)

The Italian monk and abbot St. Romuald (950?–1027) was very influential in reforming monastic life in the eleventh century. When, as a young man, Romuald witnessed his father kill a relative in a property dispute, he fled to a nearby monastery and adopted a life of penance and prayer. His example of piety, however, put the other monks to shame, and they forced him to leave — an event which helped convince him of the need for monastic reform. Romuald spent the next thirty years traveling throughout Italy, establishing monasteries and promoting the virtues of a solitary life. He had a great desire to be a martyr, and, with the Pope's permission, set out to preach the Gospel in Hungary — but was struck by a serious illness. This condition ended as soon as he halted his journey, but immediately returned every time he tried to continue. Accepting this as a sign, Romuald returned to his efforts to reform monastic life, sometimes encountering great opposition. On one occasion he was falsely accused of a scandalous crime; his fellow monks believed the accusation, and Romuald humbly accepted the punishment he was given. When a prince gave him a fine horse, the monk exchanged it for a donkey, remarking that he would feel closer to Christ on such a mount. Romuald's own father eventually became a monk in one of his monasteries; when he later wavered in his vows, his son's encouragement helped him remain faithful. St. Romuald died in 1027, and was canonized in 1595.

LESSONS

1. Sometimes, as shown by St. Romuald's mysterious illness, God gives us very clear signs that a proposed course of action — even a commendable one — is against His will for us.

2. Humility is not only essential for true holiness, but it can also help us influence others. St. Romuald's humble nature aided his efforts to reform monasticism, and even encouraged his own father to repent.

June 21 — St. Aloysius Gonzaga (Religious)

St. Aloysius Gonzaga (1568–1591) was a young man who experienced his faith as something more important than the worldly concerns of life. He lived in Renaissance Italy, a time noted for its high cultural achievements and low moral standards. Because he was born of a noble family, Aloysius was very familiar with court life, serving for a time as a page to King Philip II of Spain. The more he saw of such life, however, the less he appreciated its violent and licentious aspects. His father desired him to be a great military leader, but Aloysius, inspired by a book describing the work of Jesuit missionaries in India, decided to enter the Society of Jesus. His appalled father forbade this, and had eminent churchmen attempt to convince his son to follow a "normal" lifestyle, but Aloysius was not to be deterred. After a four-year struggle of wills between father and son, the youth was allowed to enter the Jesuit novitiate in Rome. Aloysius had to adapt himself to Jesuit discipline, which was less rigorous than that which he was already observing on his own (for instance, he was now obliged to eat and recreate more, and pray less often, than was his custom). Nonetheless, Aloysius was a model novice; he studied philosophy and had St. Robert Bellarmine as his spiritual director. The Jesuits established a hospital in Rome when a plague broke out in 1591; Aloysius was very active there in caring for the patients. He himself caught a lingering fever, but he continued his great discipline of prayer until his death at age twenty-three several months later.

LESSONS

1. Jesus said, "What profit does a man show who gains the whole world at the cost of his soul?" (Luke 9:25). St. Aloysius Gonzaga took these words to heart, and rejected the allurements of the world in order to follow Christ.

2. Sometimes parents' desires for their children are contrary to God's will; as Aloysius' life shows, a holy persistence (combined with respect for those in authority) can eventually bear fruit.

June 22 — St. Paulinus of Nola (Bishop)

The fifth century bishop and poet St. Paulinus of Nola (354?–431) was the son of the Roman prefect of Gaul (modern-day France). His family's wealth insured his rapid rise in Roman society; Paulinus became a distinguished lawyer and held several public offices, before retiring at an early age. Paulinus and his wife Therasia, a wealthy Spanish woman, were baptized in 390, and then moved to her estate in Spain. After many childless years, their prayers for a son were briefly answered — but the child died a week later. Profoundly moved by this tragedy, they dedicated their lives to God and gave away most of their property, while devoting themselves to the care of the poor. Paulinus was ordained a priest by popular demand (celibacy was not yet a requirement), and in 395 he and Therasia established a small community near the Italian town of Nola. In 409 he was chosen as bishop of Nola. During this time the Roman Empire was under increasing pressure from barbarian tribes such as the Vandals. After one of their raids, Paulinus voluntarily exchanged himself for one of his parishioners who had been enslaved. When the Vandals discovered his identity, they were amazed by such charity, and released him and all the other townspeople of Nola who had been captured. Paulinus corresponded with many of the leading Christians of the day (including Saints Augustine, Jerome, Martin, and Ambrose), and spent much time composing religious poems and hymns. He showed special concern for the poor, even arranging to give alms while on his deathbed. Soon afterwards, while lamps were being lighted for evening prayers, Paulinus said, "I have prepared a lamp for Christ," and died.

LESSONS

1. Jesus spoke of the need to "let your light shine before all" (Matthew 5:16), and St. Paulinus did this through his generosity, humility, and concern for the poor.

2. Tragedies can bring us closer to God. Paulinus and Therasia grieved over the death of their son, but also used this event as an opportunity to deepen their commitment as Christians.

June 22 — St. John Fisher (Bishop and Martyr) and St. Thomas More (Martyr)

The English martyrs St. John Fisher (1469–1535) and St. Thomas More (1478–1535) both opposed King Henry VIII when he usurped the authority of the Church. John Fisher was an important scholar who became Bishop of Rochester in 1504; he was an accomplished preacher who worked for Church reform. In 1527 King Henry wished to divorce his wife Catherine of Aragon for failing to produce a male heir, but John upheld the Church's position that the marriage was a valid one, greatly angering the king. When Henry later claimed to be the official head of the Church in England, Fisher and his friend Thomas More opposed him. Unlike the other English bishops, John refused to accept the Act of Succession, which formalized Henry's claim; as a result, he was imprisoned in the Tower of London in 1534. While there, the Pope made him a cardinal. Henry had John Fisher beheaded for treason on June 22, 1535. Thomas More, who has been called "a man for all seasons," was a scholar, author, lawyer, devoted husband and father, and civil official; he eventually became Chancellor of England (equivalent to Prime Minister), but was forced to choose between God and king. Like John Fisher, Thomas believed Henry's marriage to be valid; he resigned from his position, but the king still insisted he take an oath of allegiance. When Thomas refused, he too was beheaded; before dying on July 6, 1535, Thomas More called himself "the king's good servant — but God's first." Saints John Fisher and Thomas More were both canonized in 1935 — the four-hundredth anniversary of their deaths.

LESSONS

1. Jesus said, "Give to Caesar what is Caesar's, but give to God what is God's" (Mark 12:17). Saints John Fisher and Thomas More were both committed to this teaching — even at the cost of their lives.

2. Christians must place principle before popularity. The two English martyrs were under intense pressure to compromise for the sake of appearances, but they knew that God's truth must be upheld, no matter what the cost.

3. As St. Thomas More knew, family life should combine joy and holiness; visitors to his home were always amazed by the laughter and gaiety they found there.

June 27 — St. Cyril of Alexandria (Bishop and Doctor)

St. Cyril of Alexandria (376?–444) was a very strong-willed and controversial bishop and theologian. He was the nephew of the Bishop of Alexandria in Egypt (an important religious center), and in 412 he succeeded his uncle in this position. The early part of Cyril's episcopacy was impulsive and often violent; in his zeal for orthodoxy Cyril closed the churches of schismatics, drove Jews out of the city and confiscated their property, quarreled with the imperial prefect, and antagonized local monastic groups. However, Cyril gradually learned to control his volatile but well-meaning temper, and as he modified his abrupt ways, he provided important leadership to the Church — particularly during the Nestorian controversy. The heretical teaching of Nestorianism claimed that Mary is not the

Mother of God, but only the Mother of Christ. At the Council of Ephesus in 431, Cyril presided as the Pope's representative; Nestorianism was condemned, and — because Jesus is equally God and man — Mary was solemnly declared to be the Mother of God. St. Cyril died in 444; he is best known for his many writings on scripture and theology, and it was in recognition of these that Pope Leo XIII in 1882 declared him to be a Doctor (an eminent and reliable teacher) of the Church.

LESSONS

1. Even persons with great faults or weaknesses — such as a fierce temper — are called to holiness. St. Cyril had to change his harsh and overly-zealous style; once he did so, with the help of divine grace, he became a worthy and valuable servant of God and the Church.

2. Cyril recognized that honoring Mary is also a way of honoring her Son, and claiming Mary as the Mother of God acknowledges Jesus' divinity; this insight has always been preserved by the Church.

June 28 — St. Irenaeus (Bishop and Martyr)

St. Irenaeus (130?–202) was one of the most important theologians in the early Church. He was born in the city of Smyrna (in modern-day Turkey) and, as a youth, became a disciple of St. Polycarp. He went to Gaul (modern-day France) and, during the persecution of the Church by the Emperor Marcus Aurelius, became a priest in the city of Lyons. After becoming Bishop of Lyons, Irenaeus was instrumental in leading the fight against the heresy of Gnosticism. The Gnostics claimed that only those who had secret knowledge, and who renounced all material things as evil (including the human body), could be saved. Irenaeus opposed them by developing the concept of *apostolic succession* (in which Church teaching is guaranteed to be authentic when Church leaders can trace their authority back to the apostles), and by emphasizing the *incarnational principle* (which states that God's creation is good, and that He can use physical or material items as a source of grace). Though he vigorously opposed heresy, Irenaeus remained gentle and personally concerned for the spiritual well-being of his opponents. He is said to have been martyred during the persecution of the Emperor Septimus Severus, though details are unknown.

LESSONS

1. As St. Irenaeus realized, submission to the legitimate authority of the Church is an important way of knowing the truth and conforming ourselves to God's will.

2. According to Irenaeus, material and earthly things (money, power, authority, etc.) are not necessarily bad; they can be morally neutral, and even a source of blessing and grace when used for God's glory.

3. Even as we oppose error by correcting those who practice it and limiting their power to promote it, we must remain personally concerned with our opponents' spiritual well-being, seeking their conversion above all else, as St. Irenaeus did with the Gnostics of his day.

June 29 — Saints Peter and Paul
(Apostles and Martyrs)

Saints Peter and Paul were the two greatest apostles, and the two most important leaders of the early Church. Peter and his brother Andrew were fishermen, and followed Jesus throughout His public ministry. Saul of Tarsus (who changed his name to Paul upon becoming a Christian) was originally a Pharisee who persecuted the early Church before his conversion. Peter was largely uneducated; Paul's careful education helped him become one of the greatest religious thinkers of all history, as his numerous New Testament writings attest. Peter was directly appointed by Christ in the presence of the other apostles (Matthew 16:18–19); Paul received his authority from Christ during a personal conversion and spiritual experience (Acts 22:6–10, 14–16). Both men considered themselves to be profoundly unworthy (Luke 5:8; 1 Corinthians 15:9). Each was capable of fulfilling his mission only through Christ's grace (Luke 22:31–32; 2 Corinthians 12:7–10). Peter and especially Paul helped the Church realize that the Gospel was to be shared not only with the Jews, but with the whole world. According to legend, Peter was crucified upside-down in Rome during Nero's persecution about the year 64; Paul, as a Roman citizen, was beheaded around the year 67.

LESSONS

1. God is capable of choosing some of His servants in an "official" way (as with St. Peter), and others outside the official channels of the Church (as with St. Paul).

2. Being aware of one's personal unworthiness is per-haps a requirement in order to do great things for the Lord — and it was when Peter grew boastful that he failed most spectacularly (cf. Mark 14:29–30).

3. Human weakness is not an obstacle to God's grace; the Lord can do great things through us, as long as we remain humble and obedient — for as St. Paul said, "In weakness there is strength" (2 Corinthians 12:9).

June 30 — First Martyrs of Rome

In the first few decades after the death and resurrection of Jesus in 30AD, Christianity began spreading through-out the Roman Empire, and before long reached the city of Rome itself. Because Christians were at first considered by the Romans to be merely a sect of Judaism, they were tolerated, but the mysterious nature of the Christians' be-liefs and practices made them a target for prejudice and suspicion. In 64 a major fire devastated the city of Rome, and the rumor quickly spread that the Emperor Nero had himself ordered it so as to make room for the expansion of his palace. To divert attention from himself, Nero ac-cused the Christians. According to the contemporary his-torian Tacitus, few Romans actually believed the Chris-tians to be guilty of arson; nevertheless, large numbers of them were arrested, mocked, and cruelly tortured before being executed. Some were dressed as animals and then thrown to wild dogs for the entertainment of the crowd in the amphitheater; others were covered with flammable material, impaled on stakes, and set afire to provide light for the evening feasts Nero held in the imperial gardens; still others were crucified.

LESSONS

1. Even when Christians are innocent of sin or illegality, they may still be subject to persecution or mistreatment by state authorities.

2. Those who, by following Christ, reject the ultimate authority and values of this world, may easily find themselves resented, misunderstood, and persecuted (Matthew 24:9–10; John 15:18–19).

3. Innocence often brings out the worst in persons inclined toward evil; they may go out of their way to oppose true followers of Christ, treating them with extreme cruelty. Nevertheless, the Holy Spirit will strengthen and sustain those who are committed to Christian discipleship.

July

July 3 — St. Thomas (Apostle and Martyr)

Like the other apostles (except for Judas Iscariot), Thomas was from Galilee, and — in spite of his weakness — was committed to being a follower of Christ. Thomas is best known for his initial unwillingness to believe in Jesus' Resurrection; instead of accepting the testimony of others, he demanded to see the Risen Lord for himself (John 21:24–29). It's important to remember, however, that his statement of doubt ("unless I see and touch, I will not believe") was later replaced by an expression of faith ("my Lord and my God!"). Also, Thomas had on an earlier occasion expressed a willingness to die for Christ (John 11:16). According to legend, St. Thomas did indeed die for Christ, being martyred in southern India after spending some years there as a missionary.

LESSONS

1. God can use us, in spite of any initial doubts we may have; His grace is able to overcome our human weaknesses.

2. Spiritual growth is not a steady progression along an always-rising course; it often has ups and downs. Thomas' public statement of his willingness to die for Jesus was later followed by his abandonment of Christ (at the time the other apostles also ran away) when the Lord was arrested;

his initial doubts about the Resurrection were quickly replaced by genuine belief when he saw the Risen Lord.

3. God's grace is not limited by time and space. On Easter Sunday Jesus gave the apostles the Holy Spirit and the authority to forgive sins (John 20:22–23). Even though Thomas wasn't present, he presumably received the same spiritual gifts on that occasion (for Thomas was still considered an equal member of the apostles, but there's no mention of Jesus individually granting him these gifts on another occasion). Thus, while the Church's official actions and exercises of authority are vitally important, it's always possible for God to work in other, unrecognized, ways, as well.

July 4 — St. Elizabeth of Portugal (Queen)

St. Elizabeth (1271–1336), also known as Isabel, was the daughter of King Peter of Aragon (a kingdom in modern-day Spain), and was named after her great-aunt, St. Elizabeth of Hungary. As a child she developed habits of self-discipline and spirituality, and at age twelve was married to King Denis of Portugal. Denis was an able monarch but a bad husband, but Elizabeth forgave his notorious infidelity (which lasted for forty-one years); the queen prayed for her husband's conversion, which finally occurred on his deathbed. In the meantime, Elizabeth aided the poor and established a hospital, a home for women, and an orphanage; she also did much to promote peace among various rulers and kingdoms. When her son Alfonso led a revolt against his father, Elizabeth tried to reconcile them; Denis unjustly suspected her of treason, and temporarily banished her from court (though he later repented). After the king's death in 1325, Elizabeth retired to a convent, but in 1336 her son, by then King Alfonso IV, went to war with the neighboring kingdom of Castile. Though in extremely poor health, Elizabeth insisted on trying to make peace between the two sides; her efforts were successful, but the physical exertion led to her death soon afterward.

LESSONS

1. Jesus expects us to place Him before even our families (Matthew 10:37), but we are still called to do whatever we can to bring about peace and spiritual growth within our loved ones.

2. Sometimes our greatest sufferings are caused by those who are closest to us (especially when they don't understand or accept our mission from God — as happened to St. Elizabeth), but we are still called to love them and to pray for their conversion — no matter how long it takes.

July 5 — St. Anthony Zaccaria (Priest)

St. Anthony Zaccaria (1502–1539) was a priest who worked to renew the Church at the time of the Protestant Reformation. His Italian mother was widowed at eighteen; she raised her son to have a deep love of God and His people. Anthony studied medicine and served the poor and sick in the city of Cremona; at this time he was attracted to a religious life. He renounced his future inheritance, worked among the poor as a catechist, and was ordained a priest at age twenty-six. Sent to Milan several years later,

Anthony established two religious orders (one for men, one for women) and named them the Barnabites (after St. Barnabas, the missionary companion of St. Paul). Anthony and his followers devoted themselves to combatting a sense of worldliness and corruption which had infected the Church (and abuses of this sort had helped provoke Luther's rebellion against the papacy). Anthony preached in many churches, conducted missions, and performed public penances; his holiness prompted many people to reform their lives. While travelling on a journey, Anthony became seriously ill; he was taken to his mother's home, and there died at the age of thirty-six.

LESSONS

1. The Church is always holy (because of the Holy Spirit's presence) and always in need of reform (because of human sinfulness); each of us has a role to play in this process of reform and renewal.

2. Our example of genuine faith and holiness, lived out not only in words but in deeds, will many times prompt sinners to convert (for if they see us willing to make sacrifices for what we believe, they're more likely to take our Catholic faith seriously).

3. As shown by St. Anthony's mother, parents (even young single or widowed mothers) can play a vitally important role in helping their children travel the path of holiness.

4. God can achieve a great deal through persons fully open to His grace, even if they live very short lives (measured in worldly terms).

July 6 — St. Maria Goretti (Virgin and Martyr)

St. Maria Goretti (1890–1902) was the daughter of Italian peasants. She was not considered intelligent (and she was age twelve before being allowed to make her First Communion), but she was known for her cheerful and holy disposition. While home alone one day, Maria was assaulted by Alessandro Serenelli, an eighteen-year-old neighbor. She resisted his sexual advances, saying, "No, Alessandro; it's a sin!" Enraged, the young man repeatedly stabbed her with a dagger. Maria was taken to a hospital, where she forgave her attacker and expressed concern for her family; she died about twenty-four hours later. Alessandro Serenelli was sentenced to prison for thirty years. For the next eight years he was unrepentant, but then he had a dream in which Maria was gathering flowers and presenting them to him. Moved by this experience, Alessandro's life changed; his first action upon being released from prison many years later was to visit Maria's mother and beg forgiveness. On Christmas Day, 1937, Alessandro received communion side by side with Mrs. Goretti, and he was present in St. Peter's Square (along with 250,000 others) when Maria was canonized in 1950.

LESSONS

1. Children are capable of living virtuously and even heroically; St. Maria Goretti was canonized both because of her martyr's death (having told Alessandro that she would rather die than submit) and also because of the many simple virtues she practiced.

2. Riches, intelligence, and good fortune are not requirements for sanctity; what matters is a fervent desire to do the will of God.

3. Even the most hardened sinner can be touched by God's grace, as witnessed by Alessandro Serenelli's repentance in prison. (Opponents of capital punishment cite his conversion as an argument for abolishing the death penalty.)

July 11 — St. Benedict (Hermit and Founder)

The founder of the Benedictine Order, St. Benedict (ca. 480–547) came from a distinguished Italian family (his sister was St. Scholastica). He studied in Rome as a young man, but disturbed by the city's sinful and chaotic nature, he chose to live as a hermit at the age of twenty. Soon afterwards some monks asked Benedict to be their leader; though this initial experiment failed (as the monks were upset by Benedict's high standards, and even tried to poison him), the saint was enthusiastic over the idea of monasticism: hermits or monks living together in a community, combining contemplation, work, and shared prayer. Benedict organized twelve small communities, and in 529 established the famous monastery of Monte Cassino (with his sister establishing a religious community for women nearby). The Benedictine Rule emphasizes *ora et labora* ("prayer and work"); under Benedict's version of monastic life, a religious community devoted itself to prayer, study, and manual labor, living together under the leadership of an abbot. Benedict's rule is characterized by moderation (unlike some early Christian movements, which stressed severe acts of self-discipline), and Benedict himself, in spite of his high standards, was a gentle and peaceable man. The saint performed many miracles, and when he died, he was buried in the same grave as his sister St. Scholastica. The monasteries established under his influence played a vital role in preserving learning and culture during the Dark Ages, and the Rule of Benedict has guided many monks and religious up to the present day.

LESSONS

1. Great things can be done for God through a life properly balanced between prayer, study, and labor, with elements of solitude and community (or family) involvement, and moderate acts of self-denial.

2. Responding to God's call can be immensely more valuable than we might expect (for Benedict could never have imagined the essential role his monasteries would play in preserving Western culture).

July 13 — St. Henry (Emperor)

The son of the Duke of Bavaria (a region of southern Germany), St. Henry (973–1024) was educated by the bishop of Ratisbon, St. Wolfgang, and in 995 he succeeded his father as duke. Otto III, the Holy Roman Emperor (ruler of Germany and northern Italy), was his cousin, and upon Otto's death in 1002, Henry was elected to succeed him (though he wasn't officially crowned as emperor by the pope until 1014). Throughout his reign Henry sought to strengthen the German monarchy and to help reform and reorganize the Church. He built a cathedral in Bamberg, which later became an important religious site; he established monasteries, arranged for the care of the poor, and supported the religious reforms of his friend St. Odilo of Cluny and the other monks of the monastery at Cluny in France. Henry was particularly active in promoting Benedictine monasticism following his miraculous cure from illness at the Benedictine abbey of Monte Cassino in Italy. In all these activities Henry was supported by his wife, St. Cunegund. St. Henry was a great ruler and an example of a Christian statesman and soldier; he died in 1024, and was canonized in 1146.

LESSONS

1. Laypersons in positions of leadership and authority can play very important roles in the unfolding of God's plan, and their influence and support can be very helpful to the Church.

2. The guidance and assistance of saintly persons is quite valuable in one's own striving for holiness (for St. Henry was favorably influenced by his teacher St. Wolfgang, his friend St. Odilo, and his wife St. Cunegund).

July 14 — Blessed Kateri Tekakwitha (Virgin)

Known as the "Lily of the Mohawks," the American Indian Kateri Tekakwitha (1656–1680) was born near the banks of the Mohawk River in modern-day New York State (close to the spot where the French Jesuit missionaries Saints René Goupil, Isaac Jogues, and Jean de la Lande had been martyred a few years earlier). When Kateri was four, her parents and brother died from smallpox; she survived the disease, but it left her with a pock-marked face and partial blindness. Kateri became skilled at sewing and decorating leather moccasins and clothing, but the relatives who raised her treated her little better than a slave girl. When three Jesuit missionaries visited her village, Kateri was assigned to care for one of them. She herself was too shy to ask for religious instruction, but one of the priests, noticing her piety, came to her and spoke of Jesus. Kateri was delighted; she took instructions, and was baptized in 1676. Because she thereafter refused to work on Sundays, her relatives accused her of laziness and disrespect, and treated her severely. This, and the harsh penances she practiced, seriously affected Kateri's health, but she responded to every difficulty with love and patience. In 1677, helped by other sympathetic Indians, she escaped to a Catholic settlement near Montreal; two years later she made a vow of perpetual virginity — something unheard of for an Indian maiden. Though only twenty-four, Kateri became very weak, and died on April 17, 1680 during Holy Week. Immediately afterwards, her pock-marked face took on a new beauty, and she was buried on Holy Thursday.

LESSONS

1. The Gospel is a message of good news for every culture and people; even persons from very hostile groups can accept it and thrive on it, as did Blessed Kateri Tekakwitha.

2. Sometimes people might be eager to hear the Gospel, but too shy to ask about it (as was the case with young Kateri); thus, it's important for Christians to share it with anyone who might respond.

3. Physical beauty and attractiveness is highly prized in this world, but God is infinitely more concerned with the state of our souls. Patiently enduring physical disfigurements and infirmities, as Kateri did with the scars of smallpox, is a way of growing in grace and virtue (and the sudden transformation of her face after death reflected her far-more important spiritual beauty).

July 15 — St. Bonaventure (Bishop and Doctor)

St. Bonaventure (1221–1274) was a great Franciscan bishop and theologian. He was born in the town of Bagnorea in central Italy, and as a youth was cured of a serious illness through the prayers of St. Francis of Assisi. This, and the fact that one of his teachers at the University of Paris was a Franciscan, prompted Bonaventure to join the Franciscan Order. He remained in Paris for many years, preaching and teaching theology and Scripture; in 1257 both he and St. Thomas Aquinas (the great Dominican theologian) received the degree of Doctor of Theology. Some opponents of the Franciscans attacked the lifestyle of the monks; along with Aquinas, Bonaventure defended them, and in 1257 he was chosen general minister, or head, of the Order. Bonaventure implemented many reforms during his seventeen years of leadership, and became known as the "second founder" of the Order (after St. Francis himself). In 1265 Bonaventure was nominated as bishop of York by the pope, but declined the position. Eight years later he was appointed cardinal of Albano; his humility is illustrated by the story that, when the pope's messengers brought the red cardinal's hat to him, he asked them to hang it on a nearby tree, as his hands were still wet and greasy from doing the dishes. St. Bonaventure wrote many works of theology, philosophy, and mysticism, and died in 1274.

LESSONS

1. God's guidance is often apparent in the direction of a person's life, but we remain free to follow or reject this path; though Bonaventure was influenced by his cure through the prayers of St. Francis and by his university professor, he still could have chosen a different vocation or lifestyle.

2. Even a divinely-inspired organization such as the Franciscans can encounter opposition, for there will always be persons who misunderstand or falsely judge those who are sincerely trying to serve God.

3. Humility and holiness go hand-in-hand; had St. Bonaventure eagerly desired to be a bishop, he would have been serving himself, not God.

July 21 — St. Lawrence of Brindisi (Priest and Doctor)

St. Lawrence of Brindisi (1559–1619) was a Capuchin priest known for his great scholarship and powerful preaching. His parents died when he was a child, and his uncle arranged for him to study at the College of St. Mark in Venice. At the age of sixteen Lawrence joined the Capuchins (a branch of the Franciscan Order), and in his studies at the University of Padua he showed a remarkable facility for languages, becoming fluent in seven of them. Lawrence was ordained a priest at the age of twenty-three.

His linguistic abilities made it possible for him to study the Bible in the original texts, and he gained a reputation as a Scripture scholar. At the request of the pope, he spent much time preaching to the Jews in Italy, and his knowledge of Hebrew greatly impressed the Jewish rabbis. Though a scholar, Lawrence was also a man of action; he held a number of important positions in the Capuchin Order, and was entrusted with various diplomatic and political missions. He preached throughout Europe, particularly to Jews and Lutherans; in 1601 Lawrence gave advice to European generals fighting the Turks in Hungary, and even led troops into battle, armed with a crucifix. However, Lawrence is better known as a peacemaker; he had a great sensitivity to the needs of others, and served as a papal emissary, attempting to negotiate peace treaties between warring kingdoms. While on such a mission to the king of Spain, St. Lawrence contracted a serious illness and died on his sixtieth birthday.

LESSONS

1. Study of the Bible often makes it possible for God's servants to do great things for His glory; St. Lawrence's scholarship greatly enhanced his efforts to share the Gospel.

2. There may be times when war is necessary or appropriate, but laboring on behalf of peace is truly an even higher calling from God.

July 22 — St. Mary Magdalene
(Witness of the Resurrection)

Our knowledge of St. Mary Magdalene, one of Christ's most devoted followers, is based entirely on the Gospels, which portray her as a disciple of Jesus and as one of the women who followed and ministered to Him in Galilee (Luke 8:1–2). She was from Magdala, a small town on the northern edge of the Sea of Galilee. According to tradition, she may have been a prostitute; what is known is that she began following Jesus after He had cast out seven devils from her (this might indicate actual demonic possession, or perhaps refer to severe mental or psychological illness). After her conversion, Mary Magdalene became a devoted follower of Christ, along with her sister Martha and her brother Lazarus. She anointed the Lord's feet with costly perfume prior to His passion and death (John 12:1–8), and was present at His crucifixion. On Easter Sunday morning Mary Magdalene and two others discovered the Lord's tomb to be empty. St. Mark's Gospel states that it was to her that the risen Christ appeared (16:9), and St. John adds that she was given a message to deliver to the apostles (20:11–18). Mary was not believed at first, but her persistence prompted Peter and another disciple to investigate for themselves, thus discovering the truth of the Resurrection.

LESSONS

1. No one is beyond the power of God's grace. In spite of Mary Magdalene's sinful past, Jesus called her to repentance, welcomed her love, and treated her with respect and kindness.

2. Genuine love expresses itself in service; Mary's act of washing the Lord's feet wasn't a formality, but a true sign of her gratitude and commitment to Christ.

3. Faith helps us through times of crisis and sorrow. Though Mary Magdalene grieved over Christ's death, she continued to hope — and her faithfulness was rewarded when the Risen Lord appeared first to her on Easter Sunday, making her the first witness of the Resurrection.

July 23 — St. Bridget (Religious Foundress)

St. Bridget of Sweden (1303–1373) was a religious foundress noted for combining a life of mysticism with charitable activities in the secular world. Beginning at the age of seven, she had visions of the crucified Lord; at the age of fourteen, she was married to Ulf Godmarsson, a Swedish nobleman. They had eight children, including a daughter who was herself later canonized a saint (St. Katherine of Vadstena), and a son (Charles) who was a notorious sinner and a source of great anguish to his mother later in life. In 1335 Bridget was appointed principal lady-in-waiting to the queen of Sweden; while at court, she tried to bring about the moral conversion of the royal family. Though not fully successful at this, the king did grant her some land and buildings to use as a monastery for women. After her husband died in 1344, Bridget devoted herself to establishing a religious order for women (the Order for the Holy Savior, or "Bridgettines"). 1350 was designated a "Year of Jubilee," and Bridget decided, in spite of the Black Death, which was then ravaging Europe, to make a pilgrimage to Rome. She spent the remainder of her life there, caring for the poor and sick, giving outspoken advice on contemporary affairs to popes, writing many works describing her mystical experiences, and carrying on the work of her order, in spite of opposition and financial difficulties. While on a pilgrimage to the Holy Land, Bridget experienced shipwreck and received news of her son's death after a dissolute life. These events contributed to her own death, following her return to Rome in 1373. Her daughter Katherine completed her work by obtaining official approval for the Bridgettine Order from Rome.

LESSONS

1. Most people, even if they have great mystical experiences like St. Bridget, are nonetheless called to be active in the world, for this too can be an "arena of grace."

2. Even saints can experience difficulties and disappointments as parents; holy parents can profoundly influence their children (as Bridget did with Katherine), but there are no guarantees this will happen.

July 25 — St. James (Apostle)

James, the son of Zebedee and the brother of St. John, is called St. James the Greater (so as to distinguish him from the other apostle named James — a cousin of Jesus). Like their father, James and John were fishermen in Galilee. Soon after Jesus called Peter and Andrew (themselves fishermen and brothers) as His followers, He saw James and John mending their fishing nets; when He summoned them, they left their father Zebedee behind and became

His disciples. Though James and John deserve credit for their decisiveness in following Christ, this characteristic sometimes manifested itself as impetuousity and as a sudden temper. For instance, when a Samaritan town refused to receive Jesus, the two brothers wanted Christ to punish it by calling down fire from Heaven (Luke 9:51–56). It was perhaps for reasons such as this that Jesus gave them the title "sons of thunder." On another occasion their mother Salome tried to ensure places of honor in Jesus' Kingdom for her sons; this did not sit well with the other apostles, and Jesus patiently explained that they did not know what they were asking (Matthew 20:20–28). Along with Peter and John, James was a member of the inner group of apostles; these three witnessed the raising to life of Jairus' daughter, and also Jesus' Transfiguration and the Agony in the Garden. After Christ's Resurrection, St. James was one of the more visible leaders of the early Christian community in Jerusalem, and he was the first of the apostles to be martyred. In 44AD King Herod Agrippa had James killed by the sword to please the Jewish opponents of Christianity (Acts 12:1–2).

LESSONS

1. Passion and zeal can be very useful traits in God's service, but it is necessary to keep them under control, and to use them for God's glory, not one's own.

2. Those who act decisively in choosing to follow Christ, as did St. James and his brother St. John, will be given the opportunity to do great and valuable things in His Name.

3. As Jesus demonstrated to James and John outside the Samaritan town, our response to rejection must be marked

by love and understanding, not anger and a desire for vengeance.

July 26 — Saints Joachim and Ann (Parents of Mary)

The Gospels of Matthew and Luke trace Jesus' genealogy, but neither of them mention the Virgin Mary's parents by name, nor is there any reference to them elsewhere in the New Testament. A second century apocryphal (unofficial) writing, the *Protoevangelium of James*, professes to give an account of Mary's birth, and it is the source of the names Joachim and Ann. The accuracy of this tradition can be questioned, since many early legends relied more on religious enthusiasm than on historical fact, and since this particular story seems to be deliberately modelled on the Old Testament account of the previously childless Hannah's bearing of the future prophet Samuel (1 Samuel, chapter 1). What can be said is that Mary's parents, regardless of whether or not their names were actually Joachim and Ann, must have been God-fearing persons who provided an atmosphere which nourished Mary's perfect love and humility. Joachim and Ann can also be considered the patron saints of grandparents; though they never met their grandson Jesus while on earth, they played an important, behind-the-scenes role in preparing for the coming of His Kingdom.

LESSONS

1. Sainthood does not require fame or recognition; Joachim and Ann, though virtually unknown even today, helped prepare for Christ's coming simply by fulfilling their duty as spouses and parents.

2. Sometimes holiness involves not the performance of great deeds oneself, but loving and supporting *other* people whom God has called to do great things (as Joachim and Ann did for their daughter).

July 29 — St. Martha
(Sister of Lazarus and Mary Magdalene)

Martha, Mary Magdalene, and Lazarus were numbered among Jesus' closest friends. Martha and her family lived in Bethany, a small town outside Jerusalem, and Jesus and the apostles often visited their home. One legend states that Lazarus was very wealthy and influential, and that he and his sisters provided considerable practical and financial support to the early Church, especially after Jesus' return to Heaven. (Indeed, the legend states that the house in which the Last Supper was held actually belonged to Lazarus.) Martha is well known because of Jesus' gentle reprimand to her when she complained that her sister had left her to do the household tasks by herself: "Martha, Martha, you are anxious and worried about many things. There is need of only one thing. Mary has chosen the better part and it will not be taken from her" (Luke 10:41–42). In effect, Jesus was inviting her to discover what her sister had already learned: hearing the Word of God, and living it, is more important than any earthly consideration. Martha truly learned this lesson, for when her brother Lazarus died, in spite of her grief, she made a great profession of faith: "I have come to believe that You are the Messiah, the Son of God, the One Who is coming into the world" (John 11:27). Jesus then raised Lazarus to life, even as His own death was approaching. Because of her ministry to Christ (described in Luke 10:38–42), St. Martha is considered a patroness of homemakers and those actively engaged in the service of the needy.

LESSONS

1. Jesus calls people of many different personalities and outlooks. Mary Magdalene was (after her conversion) deeply spiritual and eager to grow in knowledge and grace; Martha was much more practical and down-to-earth. Both women were called by Jesus; both became saints.

2. There's always a need to address practical, day-to-day duties and concerns (such as the "details of hospitality" — Luke 10:40), but these must remain secondary to what Jesus called "the better part": hearing the Word of God and taking it to heart.

3. Those who believe in Jesus' promise that He is "the Resurrection and the Life" (John 11:25) will have their hopes in Him fulfilled.

July 30 — St. Peter Chrysologus (Bishop and Doctor)

St. Peter Chrysologus (ca. 406–450) was a fifth century bishop and teacher; he was given the nickname "Chrysologus" ("golden speech") because of his eloquence, but aside from a collection of homilies, none of his writings have survived. At a young age Peter was appointed bishop of the city of Ravenna in Italy, where he worked tirelessly to overcome church abuses and religious controversies. Eutyches, a heretical bishop who had been deposed for denying the humanity of Christ, sought assistance from a number of other bishops, including Peter. The saint instead upheld the Church's official teaching and the authority of the pope, and urged Eutyches to reconcile himself with the Church. Peter devoted himself to his writings and to instructing his people through his sermons, which were short, simple, and designed to relate the teachings of the Gospel to daily life. St. Peter Chrysologus died around 450, and in 1729 he was declared a Doctor (an eminent and reliable teacher) of the Church.

LESSONS

1. True holiness involves recognizing and upholding the authority of the Church Christ established, as St. Peter did when the heretic Eutyches sought his support.

2. As St. Paul wrote, "To each individual the manifestation of the Spirit is given for some benefit" (1 Corinthians 12:7). Eloquence and other God-given gifts are not ends in themselves, but must be used to further the spread of the Gospel; spiritual greatness comes from serving other people in this way.

July 31 — St. Ignatius of Loyola (Priest and Founder)

One of the greatest figures of the sixteenth century, St. Ignatius of Loyola (1491–1556) was born in Spain and served as a soldier as a young man. During a long recovery from a wound suffered in battle, he began reading the Lives of the Saints as a way of combatting boredom. Deeply moved by what he read, he underwent a profound spiritual conversion, and decided to devote his life to the service of God.

After a year of seclusion, Ignatius went on a pilgrimage to Jerusalem; he then spent ten years studying, beginning with Latin grammar among the schoolboys of Barcelona (a humbling experience) and concluding with a Master of Arts degree from the University of Paris. While in Paris, he became the leader of a group of seven students (one of whom became known as St. Francis Xavier); this group eventually journeyed to Rome and offered its services to the pope. Ignatius (at the age of forty-seven) and some of the others were ordained priests, and spent their time on various assignments from the Holy Father. In 1540 Ignatius' group was officially established as the Society of Jesus. In addition to the regular vows of poverty, chastity, and obedience, the Jesuits (as they were commonly known) made a special vow of obedience to the pope. Ignatius spent the remaining sixteen years of his life in Rome, where he established a constitution for his Order and directed its activities and growth throughout Europe. Beginning under his leadership, the Society of Jesus became one of the leading forces of Church renewal and resurgence during the Catholic Reformation. Ignatius' *Spiritual Exercises* (a guide for retreat masters and retreatants) are still in use today, and he can rightly be considered one of the greatest spiritual geniuses in the Church's history.

LESSONS

1. The lives of the saints can be a source of great inspiration and encouragement; Ignatius felt and discovered his own call to holiness after reading about the holy men and women of earlier ages.

2. Answering God's call can initially involve a period of study, preparation, and humility (as with Ignatius' ten years of formal education, including the study of Latin with schoolboys much younger than him).

3. True holiness recognizes the authority of the leaders appointed by God; Ignatius was always careful to acknowledge the spiritual leadership of the pope.

4. Living out our call to holiness can help other people discover and respond to their own call from God (as St. Francis Xavier did due to his friendship with Ignatius).

August

August 1 — St. Alphonsus Liguori
(Bishop and Doctor)

St. Alphonsus Liguori (1696–1787) was a rising young lawyer in Naples, but losing an important case prompted him to forsake the law and to become a priest instead. Alphonsus soon gained a reputation as a great preacher (though he later claimed that all his sermons could be understood by even the simplest old woman in the congregation). Alphonsus founded a congregation of priests known as the Redemptorists, a group of missionaries intended especially for work in rural areas. In 1748 he published a famous work on moral theology (a subject on which he is considered a master); he also wrote many other works intended to foster Christian faith. In 1762 Alphonsus was appointed bishop of a small Italian diocese, where he insisted upon simple preaching and a dignified and unhurried celebration of the Eucharist by his priests. Difficulties within his diocese and religious order caused him great suffering and disappointment, but he remained faithful to God and died peacefully in 1787. St. Alphonsus was especially known for his belief that sinners should be treated with patience and moderation, instead of being threatened or condemned.

LESSONS

1. Sometimes God's will for us is revealed through an apparent setback or disappointment (as with Alphonsus' loss of an important court case).

2. Writing and publishing books on faith and religion is an important ministry (and this remains the mission of Liguori Publications in Missouri, run by the Redemptorist Fathers).

3. Christians should imitate Jesus' example by treating sinners with mercy and understanding; as St. Alphonsus emphasized, this makes it easier for them to repent and to be reconciled with God.

August 2 — St. Eusebius of Vercelli (Bishop)

The fourth century bishop Eusebius of Vercelli (ca. 283–371) was born in Sardinia and raised in Rome; he served as a priest there for some years, and was appointed bishop of Vercelli, a town in northern Italy, in 340. Eusebius devoted himself to the care of the people; he was especially concerned with improving the sanctity and brotherhood of the clergy, so that they might provide the laity with a good example. He was a leader in the fight against the heresy of Arianism, which wrongly denied the divinity of Jesus. The pope sent Eusebius to the emperor to ask for a council which would end the Arian controversy; however, as Eusebius had feared, the Arians gained the upper hand, and with the emperor's support, they rejected Eusebius' demand that the Nicene Creed be accepted as a statement of Church teaching. Because of his opposition to Arianism,

Eusebius was sent into exile for six years, spending time in Palestine, Asia Minor, and Egypt, and suffering much abuse from the local Arians. Upon the election of a new emperor in 361, Eusebius was released and allowed to return to Vercelli. He worked closely with St. Athanasius of Egypt and St. Hilary of Poitiers to reduce the influence of Arianism, and he approved the Church's policy of leniency toward those bishops who had wavered in their support of the faith. St. Eusebius' final years were peaceful, and he died after a long period of service marked by a courageous defense of the teachings of the Church.

LESSONS

1. It is possible to combine a firm and unyielding defense of the truth with an understanding and forgiving attitude toward the promoters of heresy and division, as the example of St. Eusebius shows; he refused to compromise with the Arians, but was merciful toward those who repented and desired to return to the Church.

2. Those who are called to positions of leadership and service in the Church have a special obligation to provide a good example to others, especially by working together in harmony and by devoting themselves to their own personal growth in holiness.

August 4 — St. John Vianney (Priest)

St. John Vianney (1786–1859), the patron saint of parish priests, was the son of a French farmer. As a boy, he desired to be a priest, but it seemed this would be prevented by academic difficulties; however, John overcame this obstacle with the help of a tutor. He was considered a devout but otherwise unpromising candidate for the priesthood; after being ordained, he was assigned to the small town of Ars, many of whose residents were indifferent to the faith. The Curé d'Ars (Vianney's title as pastor) immediately began enduring severe fasts, many sleepless nights, and other hardships as a form of prayer for his people. He became known as a simple but effective preacher, and stories of miraculous events and powers began to circulate regarding him; Ars and the surrounding countryside soon experienced a great spiritual revival. (Not everyone appreciated him; several women had him say Mass for a "special intention" for some fourteen years. Their unmentioned intention was that he be transferred to a different parish.) John Vianney was best known as a confessor; many times he spent up to sixteen hours a day in the confessional, and he had the supernatural gift of knowing exactly what to say to penitents (reminding them of sins they had forgotten or were afraid to confess). Thousands of people from all over France flocked to his church (arousing the jealousy and opposition of some of the neighboring priests). It's said that the devil himself would often torment Vianney at night, sometimes physically beating him, but the saint would not give up his efforts to save souls. Eventually the Curé began to wear out from his rigorous lifestyle; three times he tried to leave Ars for the solitude and peace of a monastery, but the people wouldn't allow it. St. John Vianney remained at the parish until his death in 1859.

LESSONS

1. Sometimes God gives a special mission to those whom the world considers unpromising; few people considered

John Vianney a likely candidate for the priesthood (let alone sainthood).

2. Even those who are doing great things for God can expect to encounter suspicion, jealousy, and opposition (possibly from both laity and clergy).

3. Success in ministry sometimes comes at the cost of great personal sacrifice and effort (especially prayer and fasting); serving God and His people requires true dedication and commitment.

August 7 — St. Sixtus and Companions (Martyrs)

Many early Christians were martyred by the Roman Empire, including the third century Pope St. Sixtus and several other members of the Church of Rome. (August 7 is also the feast the fifteenth century priest St. Cajetan.) Sixtus was elected Bishop of Rome (Pope) in 257; that same year the Emperor Valerian issued a decree forbidding Christians to hold assemblies (thereby making it impossible for them to celebrate Mass legally). Twelve months after his election, Sixtus was arrested while addressing a gathering of Christians in a cemetery outside Rome (for the early Church could not yet legally possess its own buildings). Four deacons were also arrested, including St. Lawrence [August 10]. Sixtus and his companions were put to death by the sword; Roman Christians buried him in the nearby cemetery of St. Callistus (named after another Bishop of Rome who was himself martyred in 222.) St. Sixtus was one of the most venerated martyrs of the early Roman Church.

LESSONS

1. The Church has been persecuted in many different times and places, just as Jesus had warned (Luke 21:12–16), but has always prevailed; the Roman Empire, the most powerful force on earth for several centuries, no longer exists — but Jesus' Church remains, and will continue to exist until He returns.

2. Positions of power and influence within the Christian community are no guarantee of exemption from trouble; Sixtus, though he was Pope and a very holy man, was executed along with other Christians.

August 7 — St. Cajetan (Priest)

St. Cajetan (1480–1547) played a major role in reforming the Church during the time of the Protestant Reformation. He was born in Vicenza, Italy, and studied at the University of Padua, becoming a lawyer. For a time he worked in the Roman curia (the papal administrative offices), and then was ordained a priest at thirty-six. Cajetan established a hospital in Venice, and in his hometown he worked with a lowly religious community in caring for the poor and the sick. He soon became aware of the Church's spiritual crisis: there were many abuses, and far too many clergy were more concerned about their own well-being than with preaching and living out the Gospel. Cajetan and three friends decided to begin working for the renewal of the Church; they formed a religious congregation known as the Theatines, with a special emphasis on renewing and improving the clergy. Members of the congregation were given thorough training in Scripture (which Luther was using in a way detrimental to the Church). The Theatines represented one of several efforts of the Church to renew itself even before the Council of Trent (1545–1563); contrary to popular belief, efforts at reform were underway even before Luther's attack on Church abuses. When the Theatine house in Rome was destroyed in a war, the congregation moved to Naples; conditions were very unfavorable there, but the Theatines persevered in spite of many difficulties (and it was there that Cajetan took the unusual step of opening pawnshops — not for profit, but to help persons in temporary financial trouble). St. Cajetan continued to work among the poor, and to promote Church reform, until his death in 1547.

LESSONS

1. The Church is always in need of reform — and God provides saints and religious figures for this purpose. Those who minister in this way provide a service that is very pleasing to the Lord.

2. Cajetan did not use his great education and knowledge as an excuse to look down upon the poor or to criticize the Church for its failings; instead, he served others humbly and lovingly.

August 8 — St. Dominic (Priest and Founder)

The founder of the Dominican Order, St. Dominic (1170–1221) was born in Spain, where he was well-educated in preparation for the priesthood. Dominic was ordained in 1206, and when his bishop, Diego, was appointed a papal emissary to the Albigensians, Dominic was chosen to accompany him. The Albigensians were a heretical group in southern France who believed that all created matter is evil; they rejected Church teachings and lived simple, ascetical lives. Their lifestyle won them the sympathy of the common people, and the Church's efforts to counteract their influence had previously been unsuccessful. Bishop Diego and Dominic took a new approach; they prepared carefully for their debates with Albigensians, and themselves lived very simply. Upon Diego's death, Dominic became the leader of an effort to convert the heretics through preaching, even though the Church had previously relied on the exercise of military force by the authorities to overcome the Albigensians. In 1215 Dominic organized the Order of Preachers: a religious body of men living a simple lifestyle and dedicated to combatting heresy by preaching a message of love and forgiveness. The Order was approved by Rome in 1216, several years after the establishment of the Franciscans. (St. Dominic and St. Francis of Assisi are closely united in a number of legends, and their Orders have often cooperated closely.) St. Dominic continued travelling, preaching, and working to strengthen his Order until his death in 1221.

LESSONS

1. Evil and error (especially in matters of religion) must be opposed — but the best way of doing this is through an example of Christian love and commitment, not force. If heresy becomes attractive to people (as happened with Albigensianism), it's necessary to make the truth even more attractive.

2. Education can play an important role in serving God's people; Dominic's education helped him in his ministry (and the Dominican Order continues to play an important role in this regard).

August 10 — St. Lawrence (Deacon and Martyr)

St. Lawrence was a third century deacon and martyr in the Church of Rome. Nothing is known of his early life; as a young man, his honesty and faith prompted Pope St. Sixtus II to place him in charge of distributing Church funds to the poor. During the persecution ordered by the Emperor Valerian in the year 257, Pope Sixtus and several other Christians were arrested and put to death. [The feast of St. Sixtus and his companions is celebrated on August 7.] Knowing he himself would soon suffer the same fate, Lawrence gathered together all the Church's money and gave it away to the poor; he even sold the sacred liturgical vessels to increase the sum. Hearing of this, the prefect (a public official, equivalent to a mayor) of Rome imagined the Christians possessed a vast treasure, and he demanded Lawrence turn it over to him. The deacon agreed, asking only for three days to gather it together; he then assembled a large number of the poor, the sick, and widows and orphans. When the prefect arrived, Lawrence stated, "Here is the Church's treasure." The angry official then ordered Lawrence's immediate execution.

LESSONS

1. Stewardship is an important part of the life of the Church, for it has the responsibility of making good use of

the financial resources entrusted to it; therefore, honest and competent administrators provide a necessary and valuable ministry.

2. People are more important than things; because God has a special love for the lowly, poor and disadvantaged persons are truly a greater treasure than any amount of financial wealth.

August 11 — St. Clare (Virgin)

St. Clare of Assisi (1193–1253) was born of a noble family, twelve years after the birth of her famous townsman St. Francis, who had a major influence on her life. At the age of eighteen, Clare left home secretly and, with Francis' help, arranged to reside in a Benedictine convent. Her family's attempts to persuade her to return home were unsuccessful, and eventually she was joined by her sister (St. Agnes) and later by her widowed mother. St. Francis established the three of them as the nucleus of a religious community for women and drew up a "way of life" for them, thus establishing the Order which became known as the "Poor Clares." In 1215 Pope Innocent III granted the Order the "privilege of property": permission to live wholly on alms, without any personal or communal property or revenue whatever. (This was a privilege Clare later had to defend against good-intentioned Church officials worried about the community's well-being.) Clare was known as a great contemplative, and she provided able leadership for her community for some forty years. In spite of her own austere lifestyle, she urged others not to overdo their acts of penance, for "our bodies are not made of brass." Clare had a deep spiritual friendship with St. Francis, whom she outlived by twenty-seven years. On her deathbed, Clare was heard to say to herself, "Go forth in peace, for you have followed the good road. Go forth without fear, for He Who created you has made you holy, has always protected you, and loves you as a mother. Blessed be You, my God, for having created me."

LESSONS

1. Family and friends can play a vital role in helping us respond to God. St. Francis contributed greatly to St. Clare's holiness; she in turn inspired her sister and then her mother to answer the Lord's call.

2. We must take into account our human limitations when serving God and other people; as Clare said, "our bodies are not made of brass," so we must make a reasonable effort to maintain our health (especially by getting enough rest and nourishment).

3. If we can honestly say that we've tried to follow Jesus and to serve others in His Name, we need not fear death.

August 13 — Saints Pontian (Pope and Martyr) and Hippolytus (Martyr)

St. Pontian was a Roman Christian who served as Bishop of Rome, or Pope, from 230–235; when banished to Sardinia by the Roman Emperor, he resigned so that a successor could be elected to take his place. St. Hippolytus was a presbyter, or priest, in Rome; his name literally means "a horse turned loose," and this image accurately suggests his energy and impact — both favorable and unfavorable — on the Church. Hippolytus was a great scholar; his work *Apostolic Tradition* is the foremost source of knowledge about third century Christianity. However, Hippolytus was something of a rigorist; he felt the Church had to adopt extreme measures in avoiding the "corruption" of the world, and he thought the Church's practices in forgiving sinners were much too lax. In this he came into conflict with Pope St. Zephyrinus, Pope St. Callistus, and Pope St. Pontian. Hippolytus actually had himself elected the leader of a separate church, thus becoming the first antipope. However, in 235 he, like St. Pontian, was exiled to Sardinia, at which time (or perhaps slightly before) he was reconciled to the Church and ended his schism or rebellion. Both Saints Pontian and Hippolytus died of rough treatment in exile; their bodies were brought back to Rome and solemnly buried as martyrs.

LESSONS

1. Sometimes we must relinquish our position or authority for the greater good (as St. Pontian did by resigning, so that someone remaining in Rome might serve the community by becoming Pope).

2. There is spiritual danger in being too quick to judge others and in overemphasizing justice at the expense of mercy (as Hippolytus did at first).

3. Intelligence, education, and brilliance do not guarantee freedom from making serious errors — but greatness and holiness can be restored by admitting one's mistakes and seeking reconciliation.

August 14 — St. Maximilian Kolbe
(Priest and Martyr)

As a child, Maximilian Kolbe (1894–1941) had a deep devotion to Our Lady. On one occasion he had a vision in which Mary offered him either a white garment, symbolizing purity, or a red one, symbolizing martyrdom. "I choose both," the boy replied. Maximilian entered the Franciscan Order at age thirteen, and was ordained a priest in 1918. After serving some years as a humble parish priest, Fr. Kolbe was named director of one of the largest Catholic publishing firms in Poland. Following the German conquest of Poland in 1939, he (like many priests) was arrested, but soon released. Maximilian devoted himself to helping Jewish refugees; when the Nazis discovered this, he was again arrested and sent to the death camp Auschwitz in 1941. There he tried to set an example of faith and hope for the other prisoners. When a prisoner escaped from camp, the Germans chose ten men at random and sentenced them to death by starvation; one of them was a Polish sergeant, Franciszek Gajowniczek, whom Kolbe had befriended. Fr. Kolbe left his place in the ranks and asked permission from the commandant to take Gajowniczek's place. The shocked German officer agreed, and Kolbe and nine others were taken away to die. Maximilian helped the others prepare for death; he was the last to succumb, dying on August 14, the eve of the Assumption.

LESSONS

1. Children are capable of making a religious commitment which determines the course of their lives; St. Maxi-

milian Kolbe did indeed receive the garments of both purity and martyrdom.

2. Being a Christian may require us to work against an evil system (as Fr. Kolbe did by aiding Jewish refugees), even to the point of disobeying immoral or unjust laws.

3. As Jesus said, "There is no greater love than this: to lay down one's life for one's friends" (John 15:13).

August 16 — St. Stephen (King)

St. Stephen of Hungary (975–1038) played an important role in Christianizing his country. Stephen was born a pagan, but as a youth, he and his father, Duke Geza, were baptized by the Bohemian bishop St. Adalbert of Prague. At the age of twenty Stephen married Gisela, the sister of the Emperor St. Henry II. In 997 Stephen succeeded his father as duke, and immediately began promoting Christianity (for both religious and political reasons). After consolidating his rule, he asked the pope to confer the title "king" upon him; this was done on Christmas Day 1001. Stephen energetically guided and assisted the establishment of the Church in Hungary. He abolished pagan customs (sometimes violently, for that was the accepted manner of the age); he established monasteries and aided efforts to convert the common people. Though successful in many ways, Stephen's last seven years were bitter ones. His beloved son Emeric (also revered as a saint), whom he had carefully prepared to be his successor, was killed in a hunting accident in 1031, and his relatives shamelessly fought over which of them would be the heir to the throne (with some of his nephews actually trying to kill him). Stephen died in 1038; in 1083 both he and his son Emeric were canonized.

LESSONS

1. Worldly or political power is not necessarily an impediment to holiness, but the demands of faith must always come first (and St. Stephen demonstrated this by his submission to the Pope).

2. God's ways are not our ways, and even the careful, well-intentioned plans of saints may not be allowed to come about (for St. Emeric did not live to take the throne, as his father had hoped).

3. Personal holiness does not guarantee the respect of one's relatives or an exemption from family difficulties; what a saint accomplishes for God's glory, others may try to undo for selfish reasons.

August 18 — St. Jane Frances de Chantal (Foundress)

St. Jane Frances de Chantal (1572–1641) was born in Dijon, France; because her mother died only eighteen months later, her father (the head of the local parliament) took on the responsibility of educating her. Jane grew up to be a lovely and refined young woman with a cheerful temperament; she married Baron de Chantal and became the mother of six children (three of whom died in infancy). Jane was very happy as a wife and mother, and she devoted herself to charitable activities; after eight years of marriage, however, her husband died, and she went into a period of deep depression. Her father-in-law, a vain and stubborn old man, forced Jane and the children to live with him; he treated Jane unkindly, but she remained cheerful in spite of him. In 1604 Jane met St. Francis de Sales, a great bishop and spiritual author. He became her spiritual director, and a very warm, human, and holy friendship developed between them. In 1607 the bishop enlisted Jane's help in founding a religious order for women whose age or health prevented them from entering the rigorous lifestyle of other religious orders. Three years later the first convent of the Order of the Visitation was established, with Jane as director. Jane had much to suffer in the remaining years of her life; her religious order faced much opposition, her friend St. Francis died in 1622, and her own son was killed in a war against England in 1627. Soon after this a plague ravaged France, killing her daughter-in-law and son-in-law. Jane and her Order actively cared for the sick and the dying. Throughout this period she suffered frequent doubts and temptations against the faith, but she remained cheerful and active, establishing many other convents for her Order. St. Jane de Chantal died in 1641, and was canonized in 1767.

LESSONS

1. Cheerfulness can be a virtue; this outlook on life enabled St. Jane Frances de Chantal to attract other women to her Order and to persevere in spite of many sufferings and difficulties.

2. Friendship can be a gift from God and an aid to holiness; by becoming friends, St. Jane and St. Francis de Sales helped each other grow in grace and worked together effectively for God's glory.

August 19 — St. John Eudes (Priest and Founder)

The French priest St. John Eudes (1601–1680) founded two religious orders and encouraged devotion to the Sacred Heart of Jesus. He joined the Oratorians and was ordained a priest at the age of twenty-four. During several plagues in Normandy, he devoted himself to the care of the sick (living in a huge cask in the middle of a field, so as to avoid infecting his fellow religious). Later John began giving missions at many different parishes; his skills as a preacher and confessor made him very successful, but he noticed that the local clergy were often ineffective in their ministry, due to inadequate training. John became convinced of the need to have seminaries for the training of priests introduced on a larger scale, and he founded a new religious order — the Congregation of Jesus and Mary — for this purpose. One day a woman caring for several reformed prostitutes reproached John, saying, "Where are you off to now? To some church, I suppose, where you'll gaze at the images and think yourself pious. And all the time what is wanted of you is a decent house for these poor creatures." John was struck by these words, and thereupon formed the Sisters of Our Lady of Charity and Refuge, who actively cared for the needs of such women. John is especially known for his writings on the Sacred Heart; he presented Christ as the source of holiness, and Mary as the model of Christian life. St. John Eudes died at the age of seventy-nine, and was later declared the father of devotion to the Sacred Heart.

LESSONS

1. An especially important ministry to which some people are called is that of helping other Christians perform *their* ministry. By establishing seminaries, St. John Eudes helped insure that other priests were well-trained for parish life (and in this he accomplished even more in the long run than by the missions he gave at 100 different parishes).

2. Our faith must not be a private experience, but must manifest itself in our response to the world around us (and John humbly accepted this lesson when challenged by the woman who was caring for prostitutes seeking to reform their lives).

August 20 — St. Bernard (Abbot and Doctor)

St. Bernard (1090–1153) was an important medieval theologian and a major figure in the Cistercian Order of monks. He was one of six very gifted sons of a French nobleman. After some hesitancy, Bernard joined the Cistercian Order in 1111, persuading four of his brothers and twenty-seven of his friends to come with him. Several years later Bernard was sent to establish a new monastery at Clairvaux, which then prospered under his leadership and contributed greatly to the renewal of the Church. St. Bernard was a prolific writer, in spite of his poor health, and his widespread fame brought him into a number of the religious controversies and disputes of the age. Though personally charitable and kind, he was a formidable opponent, and he spared no effort in attacking injustice (such as excessive luxury among the clergy, or persecution of the

Jews). St. Bernard was a great theologian, and he particularly relied upon the Bible in his preaching and writing,
"not so much," he said, "to expound the words as to touch
the people's hearts." Bernard was canonized only twenty-
one years after his death in 1153, and in 1830 he was declared a Doctor (an eminent and reliable teacher) of the
Church.

LESSONS

1. As Jesus noted, holy people are often unappreciated
in their own families (Mark 6:4), but sometimes saints are
able to lead relatives and friends closer to God (and doing
so is an important ministry).

2. Poor health does not necessarily keep people from
serving God (and many times the extra sacrifice involved
makes their efforts even more pleasing to the Lord).

3. It's possible to be a fierce defender of the truth while
remaining personally understanding and charitable toward
others.

August 21 — St. Pius X (Pope)

Giuseppe Sarto (1835–1914), the future Pope Pius X,
was one of the greatest religious figures of the early twentieth century. He was born near Venice, the second of ten
children in a very poor family. Giuseppe was educated at
the village school and eventually ordained a priest in 1858
(a year before the usual minimum age). After twenty-six
years of parish work he became bishop of the Italian city of
Mantua, and in 1893 he was made Cardinal of Venice. At
the papal enclave following the death of Pope Leo XIII in

1903, Cardinal Sarto was elected, taking the name Pius X. The new pope remained very aware of his humble origins, and was embarrassed by some of the pomp of the papal court. "Look how they have dressed me up," he said tearfully to a friend. On another occasion he remarked, "It is a penance to be forced to accept all these practices. They led me around surrounded by soldiers like Jesus when He was seized in Gethsemane." (Pius and his family did have a sense of humor, however; it's said that after his mother kissed his papal ring at his installation, she then presented her hand with her wedding ring, saying, "Now you kiss *my* ring — for without it, you never would have received yours.") During his pontificate, Pius struggled with the anti-religious government of France over control of the French Church, and strongly opposed the heresy of *Modernism* (a belief that the Church should exchange some of its teachings and practices for more modern or up-to-date views). Pope St. Pius X is known for his efforts to improve the Church's worship, and especially for his encouragement of frequent reception of the Eucharist and for lowering the age at which children are allowed to make their First Communion from twelve to seven. He foresaw the coming of World War I, but to his great regret was unable to help prevent it, and died heartbroken a few weeks after the war began.

LESSONS

1. Humility and sanctity go hand-in-hand; St. Pius X was a great Pope not because of the splendor of the papal court, but because of his genuine concern for others, including children.

2. The people of many eras of history believe they are wiser than their predecessors, and that the rules and teachings of the Church are no longer needed. This error, embodied in the heresy of Modernism, is an ongoing temptation for humanity — and it is the Church's duty to oppose it gently but firmly.

3. Frequent reception of the Eucharist, which St. Pius promoted, is a vitally important element of spiritual growth and personal holiness (while also helping to build up the entire Body of Christ).

August 23 — St. Rose of Lima (Virgin)

The first canonized saint of the Western Hemisphere was St. Rose of Lima (1586–1617). Isabel de Flores y del Oliva was the daughter of Spanish parents in Peru; because her family was poor, young Rose helped support them by growing flowers and doing embroidery and other needlework. At an early age Rose was attracted by the spirituality and mysticism of St. Catherine of Siena — but her attempts to imitate her brought only opposition and criticism from her family and friends. (Rose sometimes went to what others considered extreme lengths; for instance, because she feared the admiration of her beautiful face by young men might distract her from serving God, she used to rub her cheeks with pepper to produce disfiguring blotches.) Rose's parents wanted her to marry, and for ten years they tried in vain to arrange this. Rose refused; her parents in turn refused to let her enter a convent, so she became a member of the Third Order of St. Dominic (intended specifically for lay persons) and lived at home, continuing her life of solitude and penance. A few years before her death, Rose used a room in the family home to care for the elderly, the homeless, and the sick (particularly Indians and slaves); she is today considered the originator of social services in Peru. After years of poor health and violent temptations by Satan, St. Rose of Lima died at the age of thirty-one; most of the city's inhabitants attended her funeral, with prominent men taking turns carrying her casket.

LESSONS

1. When our personal desires aren't granted, God gives us other ways of growing in holiness. St. Rose was prevented from entering the convent, but still managed to achieve a simple and holy life.

2. Family members and friends do not always understand or support our efforts to respond to God's call; as Jesus said, we must love and obey God even more than them (Matthew 10:37).

3. Holiness sometimes provokes fierce opposition from the devil (for Satan often appeared to St. Rose, threatening her and even attacking her physically), but God's grace can help us prevail.

August 24 — St. Bartholomew (Apostle)

The name of the apostle St. Bartholomew is included among the lists of the Twelve Apostles, but aside from this, there's no mention of him in the New Testament. Many scholars feel he is the same man as Nathaniel, whom St. John's Gospel has Jesus describing as "an Israelite in whom there is no guile" (1:45). Bartholomew initially doubted the possibility of the Messiah coming from Nazareth, but upon meeting Jesus he immediately declared Him to be "the Son of God and the King of Israel" (John 1:49). Early Church legends describe Bartholomew as having preached the Gospel in India and Armenia, where he supposedly suffered martyrdom by being flayed alive; the historical value of these legends is open to question. St. Bartholomew is in a sense the "unknown apostle," and for this reason, he can serve as a patron saint for almost all of us. Most of us will never become famous or important in the eyes of the world, but this matters little; all of us are perfectly known, and infinitely important, in the eyes of God. The simple, everyday lives we lead can, if we offer them to God, become ways of helping bring about His Kingdom. St. Bartholomew isn't as well known as Peter, John, Thomas, or some of the other apostles; what matters is that he responded wholeheartedly to God's call.

LESSONS

1. Jesus is not offended by our doubts, but He asks us to rise above them through our personal relationship with Him; the closer we come to the Lord, the more willing we should be to serve Him — even if we don't always fully comprehend His will.

2. Fame and recognition are not necessary in order to serve God (and in fact, they can be detrimental to our ministry); what matters is our willingness to respond to the Lord's call, even if this means working in obscurity.

August 25 — St. Louis of France (King)

St. Louis IX (1214–1270) reigned as King of France for thirty-five years. The son of Louis VIII, the young king ascended to the throne in 1235 and soon showed himself to be a just and able administrator. Louis was impartial and merciful in dispensing justice (even forgiving nobles who rebelled against his reign); he insisted on upholding the rights of each of his subjects, and sometimes held court beneath a grove of trees away from his royal residence, so that even the lowliest peasant would feel free to approach him. At the age of nineteen Louis married Marguerite of Provence (who was herself only twelve); though she was by nature arrogant and restless, she was charmed by Louis' piety and love, and they and their ten children had a happy family life. King Louis sought to bring this same harmony to France; he replaced trial by combat with an examination of witnesses, had written records kept at the royal court, and established numerous hospitals (where he himself often cared for lepers and the sick). With the exception of his involvement in the Crusades, France was at peace during his reign. Louis led an army which in 1248 captured an Egyptian port city from the Moslems, but soon afterward the Crusaders were defeated and he himself was taken prisoner. After being ransomed, Louis returned to France, but eventually led another Crusade in 1270. This was even less successful than the earlier effort, and Louis died of dysentery in the city of Tunis. St. Louis (after whom the American city in Missouri is named) was canonized in 1297.

LESSONS

1. Those who have positions of leadership and authority have a special duty to consider the needs of the poor and the lowly; "much will be required of the person entrusted with much" (Luke 12:48).

2. Our example of holiness and love can be a major source of encouragement and happiness to our loved ones; St. Louis' influence proved to be a great blessing for his wife Marguerite.

August 25 — St. Joseph Calasanz (Priest)

The Spanish priest St. Joseph Calasanz (1556–1648) devoted his life to the education of deprived children. Joseph was ordained in 1583 after being trained in canon law and theology. He went to Rome, where it seemed he had a promising Church career, but he was shocked by the ignorance and poor morals of the common people. Being unable to interest any of the city's religious orders and institutes in the education of poor children, Joseph undertook this task himself. In 1617 he and his assistants formed the Clerks Regular of the Religious Schools (the first priests to teach in elementary schools). Emphasizing love, not fear, Joseph wrote, "If from the first a child is instructed in religion and letters, it can be reasonably hoped that his life will be happy." However, Joseph himself encountered many difficulties, including his friendship with the controversial astronomer Galileo Galilei, investigations by papal commissioners, and the rebellion of one of his subordinates in the Order. Also, there were those who felt the poor shouldn't be educated, as this would only make them dissatisfied with their lot in life. Joseph was demoted at one point, and eventually his Order was suppressed, but he — like the Old Testament figure Job — remained humble and obedient. St. Joseph Calasanz died in Rome in 1648, after which his Order was finally restored as a religious community.

LESSONS

1. Education plays an important part in our Christian response to God, and a major part of the Church's mission is teaching people — particularly the lowly — of God's love for them and of their need to live in a way that pleases Him.

2. Children are often overlooked, but ministering to their needs is very pleasing to the Lord; as Jesus said, "Whoever does not accept the kingdom of God like a child will not enter it" (Mark 10:15).

3. God's servants must expect challenges, including misunderstanding and opposition; in this regard, the Lord doesn't require us to be successful, but only obedient and humble.

August 27 — St. Monica (Laywoman)

St. Monica (331–387) was the mother of St. Augustine [August 28]. Monica, her pagan and licentious husband Patricius, his cantankerous mother, and her three children (including Augustine) all lived together in North Africa. There was plenty of potential for family strife and discord, but Monica's patience and charity made the difference; her saintly example eventually brought about the conversions of her husband and mother-in-law. Augustine, however, proved a tougher nut to crack; he indulged in a free and loose lifestyle, and adhered to a pagan philosophy condemned by the Church. After Patricius died, Monica tried to discipline her brilliant but wayward son (at one point even locking him out of her house), but to no avail. Monica's constant sacrifices, prayers, and admonitions seemed to have little effect (other than annoying her son). At the age of twenty-nine, Augustine tried to break free of his mother's influence, travelling to Rome and then to Milan; a determined Monica followed him and was present when her son finally experienced a conversion. Augustine became a Christian in 387; St. Monica became ill and died soon after this. The time remaining to mother and son was short but beautiful, for they shared their faith and discussed the life to come.

LESSONS

1. A seemingly impossible family or home situation can sometimes be transformed by unfailing patience and charity — and this can even lead to the conversion of irreligious family members.

2. We must never give up praying for those who've rejected the faith, for there is always the possibility that our prayers and sacrifices will bear fruit.

August 28 — St. Augustine (Bishop and Doctor)

One of the greatest thinkers in Western history, St. Augustine (354–430) was a brilliant scholar and teacher even as a young man, but he was deluded by paganism and lived a sinful lifestyle; he fathered a child out of wedlock, and deeply resented the prayers his mother St. Monica offered on his behalf. Knowing that she wanted to accompany him when he moved to Rome, Augustine slipped away (telling her he was going down to the docks to see off a friend, when in fact he himself was departing). A heartbroken Monica followed him to Rome and then to Milan, where she was encouraged to persevere in her prayers by the great bishop St. Ambrose. The bishop's spiritual and intellectual integrity prompted Augustine to reexamine his own beliefs, and during the spiritual crisis which resulted, Augustine heard a voice telling him to "take and read" the Bible. When he did so, he opened by chance to St. Paul's statement that "the night is far spent, and the day draws near . . . therefore, put on the Lord Jesus Christ and make no provision for the desires of the flesh" (Romans 13:12–14). Upon reading this passage, Augustine finally experienced a sense of true peace and enlightenment, leading to a profound conversion. He was baptized a Christian on Easter, 387; he and St. Monica rejoiced together in the short time remaining before her death. Augustine returned to North Africa and was ordained a priest, and in 396 was chosen as bishop of the city of Hippo. He was a very successful pastor and an even greater theologian, playing a major role in overcoming the heresies of *Donatism* (an excessively harsh understanding of Christianity) and *Pelagianism* (the false belief that humans can save themselves without the help of God's grace). Many of St. Augustine's writings still exist, and he helped develop the Church's teachings on grace, original sin, and the Holy Trinity.

LESSONS

1. Sin is a reality, as Augustine himself personally experienced; however, he also experienced an even greater reality: divine grace.

2. God answers our prayers, but often in a way that demands patience on our part; St. Monica's lifelong prayers for her son were answered only a few weeks before her death.

3. A person who turns away from or rejects God, as St. Augustine did, is quite capable, with the assistance of the prayers of others, of turning back to Him and knowing Him in an even deeper way.

August 29 — Martyrdom of St. John the Baptist (Prophet and Martyr)

The birth of John the Baptist is commemorated on June 24, his martyrdom on August 29. John had been actively "preparing the way of the Lord" by baptizing and by boldly proclaiming the need for people to repent of their sins; his message was directed not only to the poor and weak, but also to the rich and powerful. According to St. Mark's Gospel (6:14–29), John had publicly criticized King Herod for living with his sister-in-law. (This was not Herod the Great, who had tried to kill the infant Jesus, but one of his sons.) Herod had John arrested and imprisoned, though he had no definite idea of what to do next. St. Mark tells us that "Herod feared John, knowing him to be a holy and upright man. . . . When he heard him speak he was very much disturbed, yet he felt the attraction of his words" (6:20). Herodias, Herod's sister-in-law, had no such respect for John; she was determined to have him killed. When her daughter (traditionally known as Salome) performed a dance at Herod's birthday feast which delighted the king and his guests, he promised to grant her anything she wanted. Prompted by her mother, the girl asked for John's head. Because of his guests, Herod reluctantly agreed, and dispatched the executioner, who beheaded John; when his disciples heard of this, they came and took away the Baptist's body, and then informed Jesus. Speaking of John, Jesus said, "Among those born of women there has been none greater than John the Baptist" (Matthew 11:11).

LESSONS

1. Responding to God's call may require us to say or do things that are unpopular with others — including people who have authority over us or who possess the ability to harm us.

2. Mere knowledge of what is good is never enough in and of itself (for Herod knew that John was holy); such knowledge must be acted upon if it is to have any meaning (and this is where Herod failed).

September

September 3 — St. Gregory the Great
(Pope and Doctor)

St. Gregory (ca. 540–604) is one of the few Church figures honored with the title "the Great," and was an important Pope and Doctor (an eminent and reliable teacher) of the Church. Gregory came from a family that had, years earlier, already given the Church two Popes. As a talented and respected young man, he was appointed prefect of Rome (an important civil position) in 572; three years later he became a monk, and eventually established six monasteries. Some time after this, Gregory was appointed the Pope's representative to the imperial court in Constantinople (the residence of the emperor). He later returned to Rome and entered a monastery, though he continued to serve as a papal advisor. When the reigning pope died in 590, Gregory — in spite of his own reluctance — was chosen by acclamation to succeed him. Though he was ill throughout most of his pontificate, Pope Gregory was an able and tenacious ruler during a period troubled by famine and the invasion of Italy by the Lombards (a barbarian tribe). Gregory acquired certain civil responsibilities (due to the collapse of civil authority in the West), and he managed to increase the power and prestige of the papacy. He sent missionaries to England, instituted reforms, restored Church discipline, and promoted monastic life. Gregory had a great influence on Church liturgy and music (one of his contributions was to codify and standardize the use of chant in the Church, this is the reason we call it "Gregorian") and his writings on moral theology and the lives of the saints were highly respected during the Middle Ages. One historian wrote: "It is impossible to conceive what would have been the confusion, the lawlessness, the chaotic state of the Middle Ages without the medieval papacy; and of the medieval papacy, the real father is Gregory the Great."

LESSONS

1. The nature of a person's vocation may change at different stages of life; Gregory served first in a civil position, then as a monk, then as a papal advisor while remaining a monk, and finally as Pope; even as Pope, his calling involved many different spiritual and secular (worldly) duties.

2. Illness is not an impediment to spiritual greatness or holiness; St. Gregory achieved many things during his papacy in spite of poor health.

September 9 — St. Peter Claver (Priest and Missionary)

The Spanish priest St. Peter Claver (1580–1654) spent his life as a missionary to slaves in the New World. He joined the Jesuit Order as a young man, and in 1610 he left Spain and went to Cartagena (located in modern-day Colombia). Peter was ordained a priest in 1616, and from then on he considered himself "the slave of the Negroes forever." Cartagena was a major center of the slave trade (in spite of repeated condemnations by the popes); each year over 10,000 slaves passed through the city after a terribly difficult and inhuman journey from West Africa (with as many as one-third dying in transit). Whenever a slave ship arrived, Peter went aboard and ministered to its miserable passengers; he also distributed food, medicine, and other necessities as the slaves were being auctioned. He realized the importance of promoting Christianity by meeting their physical needs, but he did not neglect their spiritual welfare. Peter gave them basic instructions in religion and, during his long ministry, baptized an estimated 300,000 persons. He also cared for Englishmen and other foreigners captured off marauding ships, ministered to the sick in hospitals, and even visited some of the slaves on area plantations (always staying with the slaves themselves, rather than accepting the hospitality of the owners). Peter was a moral force in the city, often preaching in the main square; though his efforts were opposed by some of the landowners, he never wavered in his commitment to the slaves. During his last four years Peter, half-paralyzed and in constant pain, was confined to one room and virtually ignored, but did not complain, saying, "My sins deserve more punishment than this."

LESSONS

1. Even if we are unable to bring an immediate end to a great evil (such as slavery or abortion), God still gives us opportunities to minister to those victimized by it.

2. Faithfully serving God doesn't guarantee popularity or even that our own needs will be ministered to (for Peter was neglected at the end of his life), but God will be with

us, nonetheless — and bearing these burdens without complaint can be an additional sacrifice for His honor.

September 13 — St. John Chrysostom (Bishop and Doctor)

St. John Chrysostom (ca. 347–407) was a famous and controversial fourth century bishop. He studied law as a young man, but then went off to the mountains for some years and lived an ascetic life; after this he became a priest and served in his native city of Antioch. It was there that his powerful and eloquent preaching earned him the nickname "Chrysostom" (golden-mouthed). In 398 John was elected bishop of Constantinople, the imperial capital. John tried to ignore politics as he exercised his ministry, but he was often caught up in controversy and intrigue. His sermons, often critical of the rich and powerful, made him many enemies, and his simple lifestyle and efforts at reform (such as deposing bishops who were mere political appointees) further alienated the ruling class. In 403 John's enemies, led by the empress and the bishop of Alexandria, charged him with heresy and misdeeds. The emperor sent him into temporary exile, but soon recalled him; in 404, however, John was exiled permanently, first to Armenia, then to Spain, where he died in 407 after several years of suffering and physical exhaustion. St. John's homilies were noted for their great scholarship and for being very practical and straightforward; he is considered a Doctor (an eminent and reliable teacher) of the Church.

LESSONS

1. Time "in the mountains" or "in the desert" (that is, a period of solitude and simplicity) can often be a preparation for a more active or dynamic mission given to us by God later in life.

2. Sometimes religion and politics are mixed together, even if we're trying to avoid this; however, the possibility of becoming politically controversial does not excuse us from the responsibility of living out and proclaiming the Gospel.

3. Scholarship is very valuable in the life of the Church — especially (as was the case with St. John Chrysostom's homilies) when it helps common people live out their faith.

September 16 — Saints Cornelius (Pope and Martyr) and Cyprian (Bishop and Martyr)

In the year 250 St. Fabian, the Bishop of Rome, was killed in a persecution; eventually St. Cornelius was elected to succeed him as pope. The Church faced not only persecution, but also opposition from within; a priest named Novatian denied the Church's authority to forgive serious sins, such as apostasy (abandoning the faith during a time of danger). Novatian even had himself consecrated as a rival bishop of Rome, thereby becoming an antipope. Cornelius, backed by St. Cyprian and other bishops, upheld the Church's teaching, and allowed sinners to do penance and return to the Church. In 253 St. Cornelius was exiled by the authorities, and died soon afterward; his gentle and forgiving manner was praised in writing by his friend St. Cyprian. A famous lawyer and orator in North Africa,

Cyprian became a Christian at age forty-six, later being ordained a priest and then bishop of Carthage. Cyprian went into hiding during the Roman persecution of 250, which allowed him to continue ministering to his people; during this time a rival priest usurped his position and then forgave all apostates without demanding any penance of them at all. This position was too lenient, and Cyprian succeeded in having it condemned by the Church. Cyprian could be gentle and forgiving, like Cornelius, but also stern and uncompromising. He was executed during a persecution in 258; St. Augustine later wrote that St. Cyprian atoned for his frequent anger and impatience by his glorious martyrdom.

LESSONS

1. The Church seeks to find a proper balance between mercy and justice: sinners must be forgiven and welcomed back, but only if they truly acknowledge their sins and show a willingness to do penance.

2. Saints can have faults (Cyprian was sometimes angry and impatient, and had trouble getting along with Pope Stephen, St. Cornelius' successor), and must continually use God's grace in overcoming them.

September 17 — St. Robert Bellarmine (Bishop and Doctor)

St. Robert Bellarmine (1542–1621) played a major role in the Catholic Reformation. Born in Italy, he was ordained a priest in the Jesuit Order in 1570. Becoming a professor at the University of Louvain in Belgium, he devoted himself to the study of Scripture and Church History, and he defended the authority of the Church against the attacks and counterclaims of the Protestants. Robert tried to take a moderate approach to the issues of the day; he upheld the Church's position and pointed out Protestant errors, but in a way which relied upon persuasion, not polemics. He argued against the "divine right of kings" (the belief that royal authority comes directly from God), thereby indirectly helping make possible modern democratic thought (and angering the kings of England and France in the process). Robert was assigned to the Roman College in 1576, and became its rector in 1592. In 1597 Pope Clement VIII made him a cardinal because "he has not his equal for learning." Bellarmine served as the archbishop of Capua from 1602–1605, and was the first to establish seminaries for the training of future priests. It was Robert who admonished Galileo when it seemed the astronomer's theories were in conflict with Scripture (though he actually defended Galileo from even harsher critics, and remained personally friendly with him). St. Robert Bellarmine died in Rome on September 17, 1621, and was later canonized and declared a Doctor (an eminent and reliable teacher) of the Church.

LESSONS

1. A study of Scripture and Church History is invaluable in defending the teachings of the Church (for, when properly understood, these sources consistently confirm and support the Catholic position).

2. Error must be opposed, but in a charitable way which allows its adherents to be persuaded by the truth; as St.

Robert knew, attacking them personally will only harden them in their position.

3. The Church must be careful not to condemn, or accept, new ideas too quickly; Galileo's belief that the earth revolved around the sun proved to be accurate, but St. Robert was also correct in insisting this theory not be automatically accepted as true until proof was presented for it.

September 19 — St. Januarius (Bishop and Martyr)

Very little is known about St. Januarius. According to tradition, he was bishop of the Italian town of Benevento and was martyred, along with six companions, during the persecution of the Roman Emperor Diocletian in 305. One legend states that he was thrown to the bears in the amphitheater of the town of Pozzuoli and, after being mauled by them, was beheaded, with his blood ultimately being taken to Naples. Not only is little known about St. Januarius, but an unexplainable phenomenon continues to keep his memory alive today. According to *The Catholic Encyclopedia*, "a dark mass that half fills a hermetically sealed four-inch glass container, and is preserved in a double reliquary [a container for relics] in the Naples cathedral as the blood of St. Januarius, liquefies eighteen times during the year. . . . this phenomenon goes back to the fourteenth century. . . . Tradition connects it with a certain Eusebia, who had allegedly collected the blood after the martyrdom. . . . The ceremony accompanying the liquefaction is performed by holding the reliquary close to the altar on which is located what is believed to be the martyr's head. While the people pray, often tumultuously, the priest turns the reliquary up and down in the full sight of the onlookers until the liquefaction takes place. . . Various experiments have been applied, but the phenomenon eludes natural explanation. Similar phenomena have been observed with the blood relics of other saints, such as Nicholas of Tolentino, Aloysius Gonzaga, and Bernardine Realino — nearly all in the neighborhood of Naples."

LESSONS

1. Christianity often provokes not only opposition, but actual hatred; Diocletian's persecution of the Church was especially severe, and St. Januarius (if the legend is accurate) and many other martyrs underwent cruel suffering and torment before actually being executed.

2. God sometimes uses unexplainable phenomena (such as the liquefaction of St. Januarius' blood, and the incorrupt state of the bodies of several deceased saints) as a reminder that the truths of faith and holiness transcend the limits of human science and understanding.

September 20 — Saints Andrew Kim Taegon and Companions (Martyrs)

September 20 is the feast of the Korean martyrs St. Andrew Kim Taegon, St. Paul Chong Hasang, and their companions. Christianity was introduced in Korea by a group of Catholic laypersons in 1784; the laity kept their faith alive until the first religious missionaries arrived in 1836, over half-a-century later. During four separate persecutions of the Church — in 1839, 1846, 1866, and 1867 — 103 Koreans were martyred, including St. Andrew Kim Taegon (the first Korean priest), and St. Paul Chong Hasang (a lay apostle). Eleven of the martyrs were priests; the other ninety-two were lay persons (forty-seven women and forty-five men). Pope John Paul II canonized the Korean martyrs during his pilgrimage to Korea on May 6, 1984; this ceremony was the first canonization in modern Church history to take place outside Rome.

LESSONS

1. The laity (ordinary men and women who are not ordained or called to be religious sisters or brothers) can play a very important role in establishing and preserving the life of the Church; it was lay persons who brought Catholicism to Korea, and who preserved it (without the benefit of the Mass or other sacraments) for over fifty years until the arrival of missionary priests.

2. Much Church History is written from a Western perspective, but it is important for European and American Catholics to remember that other cultures have much to contribute to the life of the Church, and are entitled to hear the Gospel; instead of worrying about being criticized for "cultural imperialism" (in which the Church is supposedly guilty of "imposing" its religious beliefs on other cultures), we must remember that Jesus instructed His followers to "Go and make disciples of *all the nations*, baptizing them . . . [and] teaching them to observe all that I have commanded you" (Matthew 28:19–20).

September 21 — St. Matthew
(Apostle and Evangelist)

St. Matthew, one of the Twelve Apostles, was originally a tax collector in the city of Capernaum. Many local tax collectors (known as publicans) were corrupt, demanding more money from the people than the Romans required and keeping the difference for themselves; this, and their apparent lack of patriotism, made them hated figures in first century Palestine. We don't know whether Matthew was personally dishonest, but we do know he eagerly accepted Christ's invitation. The call of Matthew is described in St. Mark's Gospel (2:13–17). Matthew, also known as Levi, the son of Alphaeus, was at his tax collector's post when Jesus said to him, "Follow Me." Matthew did this, without a moment's hesitation; later, Matthew invited Jesus and the disciples to dine at his home. Our Lord's acceptance caused great rejoicing among Matthew's friends (themselves tax collectors, prostitutes, and sinners). When the Pharisees objected, Jesus said, "I have come to call sinners, not the self-righteous." Matthew, to whom authorship of the First Gospel is traditionally assigned, was present for all the major events of Christ's life. Little or nothing is known about St. Matthew's life after Jesus' death and resurrection. There are various and conflicting legends regarding his missionary activity and subsequent martyrdom (Ethiopia and Persia are two of the places mentioned as sites of his death).

LESSONS

1. All people are important in God's eyes and capable of great sanctity — even those despised by society and considered hopeless sinners.

2. Accepting someone in Christ's Name may also lead to the conversion of that person's family and friends; Matthew introduced Jesus to many of his friends and colleagues (persons who, because of their status as public sinners, probably would not otherwise have had the chance to meet Our Lord).

3. Some persons, such as St. Matthew the Evangelist (the author of the Gospel), are given the gift of writing; when this ability is used for God's glory, it can bring about conversion and make a lasting difference in the lives of many people.

September 26 — Saints Cosmas and Damian (Martyrs)

The martyrs Cosmas and Damian were executed in the city of Cyrrhus in Syria about 303, during the persecution decreed by the Roman Emperor Diocletian. Aside from this, nothing is known about their lives with any certainty. An early legend, however, suggested that they were twin brothers born in Arabia who became skilled physicians. As Christians, according to the legend, they charged no fees of those they healed or cared for; they were thus called "the holy moneyless ones," and along with St. Luke (the "beloved physician" mentioned by St. Paul in Colossians 4:14), Cosmas and Damian are considered the patron saints of doctors. Within a century of their death, their fame had spread more widely than that of most martyrs, and perhaps as early as the sixth century their names were added to the Roman Canon (the source of our current Eucharistic Prayer [no. 1] used at Mass).

LESSONS

1. Most of the people now in Heaven (all of whom can technically be called "saints") are unknown to history, and there are some, such as Cosmas and Damian, about whom very little is known to us today. What matters, however, is that they are known to God; their names are listed in the scroll of history given to the Lamb (Revelation 5:7) and are recorded in the Book of Life (Revelation 20:15). Thus, we should seek to please God — even if we're laboring in relative obscurity — instead of trying to become famous or make a name for ourselves in the world.

2. Caring for the sick, as Saints Cosmas and Damian did (assuming the legend is true), is an important part of the Church's mission; meeting the immediate, physical needs of others makes it easier for them to believe in God's eternal, spiritual love for them.

September 27 — St. Vincent de Paul (Priest and Founder)

The name of the French priest St. Vincent de Paul (ca. 1580–1660) is today synonymous with charitable activities on behalf of the poor. Vincent was the son of a peasant farmer, and was ordained at the relatively early age of twenty. For the next ten years, Fr. Vincent was content with an unchallenging, comfortable life in the bosom of the Church. Then, however, he came under the influence of the saintly Fr. de Berulle, and began to work among the poor. Their material and spiritual needs moved Vincent profoundly, and from then on he devoted himself to serving the forgotten members of society. Fr. Vincent arranged for groups of lay persons to minister to the poor, and in 1625 he founded the Congregation of the Mission (also known as the Vincentians), a group of priests who dedicated themselves to working with members of small towns and villages. In 1633 Vincent, along with St. Louise de Marillac, founded a congregation of religious women known as the Daughters of Charity. Vincent's generosity and goodness attracted many people, and he had little difficulty finding helpers for his ministry. A gentle manner was not something that came easily to him, however; he had a severe temper, and stated that, without the grace of God, he would have been "hard and repulsive, rough and cross." St. Vincent de Paul died in Paris in 1660, and was canonized in 1737. Pope Leo XIII made him the patron of all charitable activities in the Church, particularly the Society of St. Vincent de Paul, which was founded in 1833 by Frederic Ozanam.

LESSONS

1. Sometimes God may grant us a safe and comfortable stage of life, but we shouldn't assume this is the normal or permanent state of affairs; the Lord may have a great spiritual challenge in store for us.

2. An important way of serving Christ is making it possible for others to minister in His Name, as St. Vincent de Paul did by recruiting lay assistants and establishing religious orders.

3. A gentle and loving personality doesn't always happen automatically as one grows in holiness; sometimes an ongoing effort, and the constant help of divine grace, is required to grow in this regard.

September 28 — St. Wenceslaus (King and Martyr)

St. Wenceslaus (ca. 907–929) is the patron saint of the Czech Republic. He was born early in the tenth century near the city of Prague, the son of the Duke of Bohemia. Wenceslaus was raised by his grandmother, St. Ludmilla, who tried to promote him as the ruler of Bohemia instead of his mother Drahomira, who supported anti-Christian groups in the kingdom. In 921 Ludmilla was murdered, but the Christian forces were nonetheless successful in the political intrigues which followed, making it possible for Wenceslaus to ascend the throne. The young king tried to unify Bohemia, support the Church, and negotiate peace with Germany; unfortunately, his efforts met bitter opposition. Wenceslaus' own brother Boleslav was involved in the intrigues against him. Boleslav invited his brother to attend a Mass with him, while secretly plotting an ambush. On the way to church Wenceslaus was killed by his brother's supporters. Though both St. Ludmilla and St. Wenceslaus were killed as a result of political intrigues, and not religious persecution, they were nonetheless acclaimed as martyrs. St. Wenceslaus is a national hero in Bohemia; the fa-

mous Christmas carol about him (written by J. M. Neale)
actually has nothing to do with his life.

LESSONS

1. It is important for children and young people to be
guided and taught by committed Christians, as St. Wenceslaus was by his grandmother; this can counteract other, un-
healthy spiritual influences in the home (as represented by
Wenceslaus' mother and brother).

2. Personal holiness is no guarantee of safety or of success in the political realm; in one way or another all Christians must take up their cross each day and follow in the
Lord's footsteps.

September 29 — Michael, Gabriel, and Raphael (Archangels)

The archangels Michael, Gabriel, and Raphael are honored on September 29; October 2 is the Feast of the
Guardian Angels. Michael has been widely venerated by
Jews and Christians alike, and because of a passage from
the Book of Revelation describing him as leading the angels in the war against Satan and his followers (12:7–9),
Michael is considered the patron saint of soldiers. Gabriel
is the archangel who appeared first to Zechariah and announced the conception of John the Baptist (Luke 1:10–20),
and then to Mary to announce God's plan to make her the
mother of the Savior (Luke 1:26–38). Raphael is the angel
who cured the Old Testament hero Tobit of his blindness
(Tobit 11:7–15). St. Gregory the Great (Pope from 590–
604) wrote: "You should be aware that the word 'angel'

denotes a function rather than a nature. Those holy spirits of Heaven have indeed always been spirits They can only be called angels when they deliver some message. More-over, those who deliver messages of supreme importance are called archangels. . . . Some angels are given proper names to denote the service they are empowered to perform. . . . Thus, Michael means 'Who is like God?'; Gabriel is 'The Strength of God'; and Raphael is 'God's Remedy.' "

LESSONS

1. The existence of angels has been a constant teaching of the Church; in addition to their great power and intel-ligence, these spiritual beings have an immense love for us and are pleased to serve and assist us as part of God's plan.

2. Scripture tells us that God has assigned angels to guide and protect us (Matthew 18:10; Psalm 91:11–12; Acts 12:15), so we shouldn't hesitate to pray for their intercession and assistance.

September 30 — St. Jerome (Priest and Doctor)

St. Jerome (ca. 345–420), one of the greatest scholars in the Church's history, thoroughly studied language and Scripture; he went to Antioch and learned Hebrew from a Jewish rabbi, and then to Constantinople, where he studied under St. Gregory of Nazianzus. He was ordained a priest, and from 382–385 served as secretary to Pope St. Dama-sus in Rome. The Pope directed him to produce a Latin version of the Bible (Latin being the language of the com-mon people). Jerome labored a long time on this project, translating the Old Testament from Hebrew and the New

Testament from Greek. The finished version was known as the Vulgate (from the Latin *vulgus*, meaning common, or for common people), and it remained the Church's official translation for well over a thousand years. While in Rome, Jerome became the leader of a group of persons attracted to a penitential life, but his harsh and demanding nature made him as many enemies as friends, and after Pope Damasus' death, Jerome returned to the East, followed by St. Paula, St. Eustochium, and other of his disciples. They established a religious community in Bethlehem, with a hospice for travelers and a school for children (in which Jerome himself taught Greek and Latin, even as he continued his scholarship). Jerome was uncompromising against heresy, and was known for his fierce temper; his writings were sometimes sarcastic or vitriolic, but at the same time he was gentle with the poor and downtrodden, and his awareness of his weaknesses prompted him to perform great acts of penance (such as living in a cave until his death). His contemporary St. Augustine said of him, "What Jerome is ignorant of, no mortal has ever known."

LESSONS

1. Scholars who make Scripture and Church teaching accessible to common people provide an important service to the Church; this was true of St. Jerome and other saints (such as St. John Chrysostom [September 13].

2. Awareness of our moral and spiritual weaknesses obligates us to perform penance and to cultivate virtues so as to overcome our faults; in order to tame his temper, St. Jerome lived very simply and, in spite of his great reputation and the demands of scholarship, made a point of being friendly and accessible to children and the poor.

October

October 1 — St. Thérèse of Lisieux (Religious)

One of the Church's most popular saints is Thérèse of Lisieux (1873–1897), known also as Thérèse of the Child Jesus. She was a Carmelite nun who lived a cloistered life in the convent of Lisieux, France. Four of her sisters were themselves nuns, and she entered the convent at the age of fifteen (joining two of her sisters at Lisieux). Her nine years there were uneventful and ordinary, yet also heroic. Thérèse realized that sanctity could be achieved even in and through the simple routines of life. Instead of ambitiously seeking to do great things, she contented herself with following her "little way": simple trust in and love for God, and the attempt to glorify Him in everything she did, no matter how insignificant. She once said, "I prefer the monotony of obscure sacrifice to all ecstasies. To pick up a pin for love can convert a soul." Thérèse suffered from poor health all her life; in spite of her frailty, she spent many hours of hard work in the convent laundry and refectory. During her last year of life, she contracted tuberculosis and suffered greatly before dying at the age of twenty-four. (The day of her death she murmured, "I would not suffer less.") Her autobiography, written in obedience to her superiors, was later published under the title *The Story of a Soul*.

LESSONS

1. St. Thérèse is attractive to many people because her understanding of holiness is very practical: simply doing everything, no matter how routine, with as much love as possible.

2. As the Second Vatican Council emphasized, *all* Christians are called to holiness. This doesn't have to involve religious adventures, spiritual ecstasies and visions, or heroic deeds; instead, we can glorify God and grow in grace simply by fulfilling our daily duties faithfully and lovingly.

October 4 — St. Francis of Assisi (Founder)

St. Francis of Assisi (1181–1226), one of the best-known and most-loved saints of history, was the son of a wealthy merchant in the Italian town of Assisi. At first he was a carefree youth, but then became convinced of the need to find a deeper meaning in life; he discovered this by trying to live out the Gospel completely, in a joyful and humble manner. Hearing Christ tell him to "repair My falling house," Francis sold some goods from his father's warehouse and used the proceeds to reconstruct the dilapidated church of San Damiano. An angry father disowned and disinherited him, and Francis thereupon adopted a life of poverty. His simple and sincere faith attracted many followers, and in 1210 Pope Innocent III authorized Francis and his companions to travel about Italy, preaching the Gospel. (The Pope's favorable decision is said to have been influenced by a dream in which he saw Francis supporting a crumbling church.) Francis and his followers, known as the Friars Minor (and later as the Franciscans), devoted themselves to poverty, penance, and preaching, and their efforts contributed to a major spiritual renewal in thirteenth century Italy. In 1212 Francis aided his friend St. Clare of Assisi in establishing an order for women; later he travelled to the Holy Land in an unsuccessful attempt to convert the Moslems. Francis is especially known today for his gentleness and his great love for all God's creation, especially animals and nature. Though never ordained a priest, Francis was blessed with many spiritual gifts, particularly the stigmata (wounds in the hands, feet, and side like those suffered by Christ on the cross). During his last two years of life, when he was half-blind and seriously ill, Francis remained joyful and humble; he died at the age of forty-four, and was canonized only two years later.

LESSONS

1. True joy comes not from earthly status and success, but from following Christ as completely as possible — and many others can be attracted to Jesus by our efforts to live out the Gospel.

2. As St. Francis realized, poverty, or a simple lifestyle, can be a great blessing, for it allows us to "store up treasures in Heaven" (Matthew 6:20).

3. God is pleased when we cherish and appreciate all the elements of His creation.

October 6 — St. Bruno (Priest and Founder)

The founder of the Carthusian Order of hermits, St. Bruno (ca. 1033–1101) was born in Cologne of a noble family; he studied in the cathedral school of Rheims, and after being ordained a priest, taught theology there for the next twenty years. During this period, Pope Gregory VII was trying to reform the Church; in particular, he sought to end the custom by which kings and feudal lords appointed men of their own choosing to be bishops. (Unworthy men often sought important offices in the Church because of the economic and political benefits involved.) Bruno supported the Pope's efforts, and himself played a major role in deposing the archbishop of Rheims, who had obtained the position through bribery; as a result, the archbishop's henchmen ransacked Bruno's room and had him dismissed from his teaching position. Bruno had long dreamt of a life of prayer and contemplation in solitude, and in 1084 he and some friends accepted a gift of land in Grand Chartreuse, an isolated area near Grenoble. A small church and several simple huts were built, and the hermits, soon known as Carthusians (after the region), began a combination of solitude and communal living which has remained unchanged to this day (and which, unlike the experience of most religious orders, has never had to be modified significantly or reformed). The hermits devoted themselves to a life of worship, private and communal prayer, and penance; their primary work was that of copying and preserving manuscripts. Pope Urban II, one of Bruno's former students, called him to Rome to be his advisor. Though not wishing to leave the eremitic lifestyle, Bruno obeyed; however, he was able to establish several hermitages in Italy, and he remained there until his death in 1101. Because the Carthusians shun all ecclesiastic honors and publicity, St. Bruno was never formally canonized, but his feast is nonetheless celebrated throughout the Church.

LESSONS

1. The need for reform is an ongoing reality in the Church because of the human weakness and sinfulness of its members; however, God always provides saints and leaders for this effort.

2. What may seem to be a setback can actually be an opportunity; when St. Bruno was unfairly dismissed from his teaching position, this allowed him to pursue his dream of a eremitic life.

3. Great things can come from a proper balance of solitude, communal living, prayer, and work; the Carthusian Order has been a continuing source of grace and blessing for the Church.

October 9 — St. Denis (Bishop and Martyr) and Companions

October 9 is the feast of St. Denis and his companions (and also of an Italian priest of the sixteenth century named St. John Leonardi). Denis (also known as Dionysius) was the first bishop of Paris, and is commonly considered one of the patron saints of France. He lived in the third century; little is known about him, though there are many conflicting (and even unlikely) legends about his life. It is said that, in the year 250, Denis was sent to Gaul (the Ro-

man name for France) with several other missionaries. He
served as the bishop of Paris until the persecution launched
by the Emperor Valerian in 258. At that time Denis, a priest
named Rusticus, and a deacon named Eleutherius, were beheaded in the section of Paris known today as Montmartre
(which means "Martyrs' Hill").

LESSONS

1. Many of the saints travelled far from their homelands,
living (and in the case of some martyrs, dying) in foreign
lands. St. Denis and his fellow missionaries, for instance,
were not native to Gaul, but it was there that they served
Christ. We are "home" on earth when we're serving Christ
in the place God calls us to be — and this helps prepare
us to enter our true home of Heaven.

2. "The blood of martyrs is the seed of future Christians." Today Montmartre is the site of one of the holiest places in France — the basilica of Sacre Coeur (Sacred
Heart), where people from around the world participate
in perpetual eucharistic adoration.

October 9 — St. John Leonardi
(Priest and Founder)

The Italian priest St. John Leonardi (ca. 1541–1609) was
known for caring for the poor, the sick, and the imprisoned. His example of faith and dedication attracted several
other young men; they began to assist him, and were eventually ordained priests themselves. John and his followers
sought to establish a confraternity of diocesan priests to

work among the poor, with an emphasis on teaching them the truths of the faith. (This was part of the Church's re sponse to the Protestant Reformation.) John's Order, the Clerks Regular of the Mother of God, was eventually approved by the Church, but it provoked violent political opposition, and for most of his life John was exiled from his hometown of Lucca. During John's difficulties, he was assisted and encouraged by St. Philip Neri [a popular Roman priest whose feast is celebrated on May 26]. Philip shared his quarters with John (even placing him in charge of caring for his cat!). In 1579 John established the Confraternity of Christian Doctrine (the origin of CCD, or religious education, classes); he wrote a simple pamphlet of Catholic belief which has remained in use for over two centuries. In 1595 Pope Clement VIII gave official approval to John's Order, which, even though small (as it deliberately remains today), provided excellent services to the Church in Italy. In 1609 St. John Leonardi caught the plague while tending the sick, and died soon afterward; he was canonized in 1938.

LESSONS

1. Just as Jesus became unpopular in His hometown of Nazareth (Luke 4:16–30), those who follow Him may be exiled from or unwelcome in their homes — as happened to St. John Leonardi.

2. The Church's mission involves responding both to physical needs (as illustrated in St. John's care of the sick and the poor) and to spiritual needs (demonstrated by his efforts to teach the faith); this reflects the truth that Christ's followers are in this world but not truly of the world (John 17:16).

October 14 — St. Callistus (Pope and Martyr)

St. Callistus was one of the most unlikely, yet highly influential, Popes of the early Church. He was originally a slave in an important Roman household. Callistus managed to lose some money entrusted to his care, so he fled; upon being recaptured, he was imprisoned for a time. Soon after his release, he was arrested again (this time for causing a disturbance in a Jewish synagogue), and sentenced to work in the mines of Sardinia. Eventually Callistus was freed through the influence of a member of the imperial court. After being emancipated from slavery, Callistus was placed in charge of the public Christian burial ground in Rome; this land, which is still known as the cemetery of St. Callistus, was possibly the first property ever owned by the Church. Pope St. Zephyrinus ordained Callistus a deacon and relied upon him as an advisor; after the Pope's death in 217, Callistus was chosen to succeed him as the sixteenth Bishop of Rome. This provoked a schism, for St. Hippolytus, the losing candidate, established himself as the first antipope and bitterly attacked Callistus' positions. Especially galling to Hippolytus was Callistus' willingness to readmit notorious sinners to the Church upon sincere repentance and acts of penance. (Hippolytus, a very strict and demanding person, felt the Pope was being much too lenient.) In 222 Callistus was killed, probably by a rioting mob, and he was soon venerated as a martyr. Most of the information we know about him comes from St. Hippolytus (who was reconciled to the Church before dying as a martyr in 235 [August 13]).

LESSONS

1. We must never write off anyone as hopeless, for God can use people who, in the world's eyes, are lowborn, incompetent, and troublemakers; Callistus was, or appeared to be, all these things — yet he became a great saint.

2. Practical Christianity requires a balance between high moral ideals, on the one hand, and mercy and understanding toward those who fall short, on the other; St. Callistus — perhaps aided by memories of his own stormy past — strove to achieve such a balance.

October 15 — St. Teresa of Avila (Virgin and Doctor)

St. Teresa (1515–1582) was born in Avila in Spain, and was raised in a warm and loving family. She herself was known for her engaging personality; she was beautiful, outgoing, enthusiastic, and courageous. At the age of twenty, though reluctant to give up family life, she entered the Carmelite convent in Avila. For a time she became seriously ill, but she persevered in her vocation, and over the years she had many deep mystical experiences. Teresa was capable of very deep meditation, and she did much writing on the subject, but she remained a very practical, down-to-earth person. The Carmelite Order had originally followed a very strict rule, but it had gradually fallen away from this. Teresa, encouraged by St. Peter Alcantara and others, resolved to establish a new branch of the Order and to observe the original rule. After many difficulties, a convent was opened in Avila in 1562. Teresa and her followers became known as "Discalced" (barefooted) Carmelites, as they observed the rule's original prohibition against shoes. Teresa established other convents and promoted religious reform; she managed to unite a life of deep spirituality and prayer with constant activity. The best known of her writings is *The Interior Castle*, in which she describes different stages of spiritual growth. She was canonized forty years after her death in 1582, and in 1970 she and St. Catherine of Siena became the first women to be declared Doctors (an eminent and reliable teachers) of the Church.

LESSONS

1. Having a warm, enthusiastic personality is no impediment to holiness; St. Teresa greatly enjoyed life and activities with her family, even as she was called to a religious vocation.

2. Religious activity must be nourished by prayer and meditation; it was precisely because St. Teresa spent so much time in prayer that she had the energy to reform the Carmelite Order, establish convents, and write important scholarly works.

October 16 — St. Hedwig (Duchess)

The feast of the Bavarian duchess St. Hedwig (1174–1243) is celebrated on October 16. (This date is also the feast of St. Margaret Mary Alacoque.) Hedwig was known for her many charitable activities. She was the daughter of a German count, and was the aunt of St. Elizabeth of Hungary (a Hungarian princess [November 17]). Hedwig was married at an early age to Henry, Duke of Silesia. Her husband was a religious man who encouraged her many works of charity; through their efforts, monastic institutions for both men and women were established, along with hospitals and homes for the poor. Hedwig and Henry had six children. After Henry died in 1238, Hedwig resided in the convent of Trebnitz (where her daughter Gertrude was abbess) and became part of the community there. However, Hedwig did not become a nun, as this would have meant relinquishing the family estates; she preferred to retain control, thus insuring that her family's wealth would be used for the ongoing care of the poor and needy. St. Hedwig died at the convent of Trebnitz in 1243, and was canonized in 1267.

LESSONS

1. One of the purposes of marriage is the mutual sanctification of the spouses; husbands and wives should help one another grow in holiness. St. Hedwig and her husband Henry exemplify this truth; their mutual support and encouragement helped each other (and their children) grow in grace.

2. Being a wife and mother (or a husband and father) isn't necessarily an obstacle to holiness; rather, for those called to marriage and parenthood, it is the "arena" in which spiritual growth can and should occur.

3. Sometimes practical considerations can legitimately be given priority (as when St. Hedwig chose not to become a nun in order to continue overseeing the proper use of her family's material resources).

October 16 — St. Margaret Mary Alacoque (Virgin and Religious)

The visions of Christ granted to St. Margaret Mary Alacoque (1674–1690) led to the Church's formal veneration of the Sacred Heart of Jesus. Margaret Mary's childhood in eastern France was unhappy because of family problems and illness; after briefly considering marriage, she entered the Order of Visitation Sisters at the age of twenty-four. She was considered a simple and undistinguished nun; though she was humble and patient and open to criticism or correction, her superiors considered her clumsy and somewhat slow, and she had difficulty in meditating in the formal way expected of the sisters. On December 27, 1674, Margaret Mary experienced a vision or apparition of Christ. Jesus showed her His Sacred Heart, a symbol of His often-rejected love for humanity, and asked her to promote devotion to His Sacred Heart through frequent Communion and an hour of prayer each Thursday night (in memory of His agony in Gethsemane). Christ appeared to Margaret Mary on four separate occasions; when others learned of the visions, they accused her of delusions or deliberate fraud. However, her Jesuit confessor, St. Claude la Colombiere, supported and encouraged her. Margaret Mary's gentleness and patience convinced many people of the genuineness of the apparitions, and the Feast of the Sacred Heart of Jesus was eventually established in 1856.

LESSONS

1. Throughout history God has made a point of choosing those considered least suitable by the world. St. Margaret

Mary wasn't highly thought of within her own convent, but it was precisely her humility and simplicity which allowed Jesus to reveal to her the depth of love found within His Sacred Heart.

2. Many people claim to receive visions, and it's difficult to discern the true from the false. As Jesus said, "By their fruits you will know them" (Matthew 7:20) — and the fruits of St. Margaret Mary's holiness convinced the Church of the authenticity of her spiritual experiences.

October 17 — St. Ignatius of Antioch
(Bishop and Martyr)

St. Ignatius of Antioch was an important bishop who suffered martyrdom early in the second century. Little is known of his life. He was probably born in Syria; according to an unlikely legend, he was the child whom Jesus placed in the midst of His disciples to teach them humility (cf. Matthew 18:1–4). Legends of greater reliability state that he was a disciple of Saints Peter and Paul, or possibly of St. John. Ignatius eventually became the second or third bishop of Antioch, an important Syrian city and a major center of early Christianity. During a persecution the Christians were ordered to deny their faith, under pain of death. Ignatius, by then an old man, refused to do this, and as a well-known Christian, he was sentenced to die in Rome itself. On the journey to Rome he was escorted by a squad of soldiers; he referred to them as "ten leopards," and noted that their behavior "gets worse the better they are treated." During this period he wrote seven famous letters or epistles; six of them were letters of exhortation to vari-

ous Christian communities, and the seventh was a letter of
pastoral advice to St. Polycarp [February 23], whom he met
shortly after his arrest. In these writings Ignatius urged the
Christian communities to remain faithful to their bishops,
as this was essential to preventing heresy and division. In
his letter to the Christians of Rome, Ignatius begged them
not to work for his release, for he deeply desired to die
as a witness to the faith. When Ignatius arrived in Rome
during or soon after the year 107, he was thrown to the
lions in the Coliseum, meeting his death bravely.

LESSONS

1. From the earliest days of the Church there has been
a recognition of the need for authority and structure; St.
Ignatius stressed that only in this way can anarchy and
religious confusion be avoided.

2. In his "Letter to the Trallians," St. Ignatius wrote:
"Never give the pagans the slightest pretext, so that the
great majority who serve God will not be mocked because
of the folly of a few." As members of Christ's Body, we
must remember that outsiders may very well be judging
the entire Church based on our example — and so we have
a great responsibility in this regard.

October 18 — St. Luke (Evangelist)

St. Luke lived in the first century, and is considered the
author of the Gospel of Luke and the Acts of the Apostles.
Luke was a Gentile, making him the only non-Jewish author in the entire New Testament; he had a Greek back-

ground and education, and may have been born in Antioch. He is often identified as a doctor, for St. Paul referred to him as "our beloved physician" (Colossians 4:14). The latter part of the Acts of the Apostles (beginning with 16:10) is written in the first person, suggesting that Luke accompanied Paul on some of his missionary journeys. Paul himself referred to Luke on several occasions, stating in one of his letters to Timothy that Luke was at that time his only companion (2 Timothy 4:11). Scholars are unsure when Luke wrote his Gospel; it is commonly dated between 75–85AD, though some experts hold for an earlier date of composition. Luke's Gospel is a Gospel of Mercy; it emphasizes Jesus' identification with the poor and the lowly, and His willingness to forgive sinners. At the same time, it is a demanding Gospel, for it shows that being a follower of Christ requires sacrifice and commitment. Luke was such a follower, for he faithfully used his literary talents to help share the Good News of salvation.

LESSONS

1. As a Gentile (non-Jew), St. Luke brought a unique and valuable perspective to the New Testament, particularly in reminding his readers that Jesus loves everyone (including women, children, sinners, the poor, and Gentiles) and that He came for the salvation of all people.

2. Holiness sometimes requires us to be both gentle and uncompromising. The Gospel of Luke shows a warm and loving Jesus Who nevertheless expects His followers to give up everything for Him.

October 19 — St. Isaac Jogues and Companions (Missionaries and Martyrs)

The French Jesuit priests St. Isaac Jogues (1607–1646), St. John de Brebeuf (1593–1649), and their companions St. John de Lalande, St. René Goupil, St. Anthony Daniel, St. Charles Garnier, St. Gabriel Lalemant, and St. Noel Chabanel were among the first missionaries to the North American Indians, and were the first martyrs of North America. Isaac Jogues became a Jesuit in 1624, and in 1636 he travelled to Quebec as part of a group of missionaries under the leadership of John de Brebeuf. They managed to convert some of the Hurons, but in 1642 Isaac Jogues, several other missionaries, and some of their Huron converts were captured by an Iroquois war party. The Jesuits were tortured, and the Huron Christians murdered. Isaac Jogues escaped and returned to France, where he was welcomed as a hero, but he desired to continue his missionary work in the New World. He returned to North America, and in 1646 he and St. John de Lalande were captured by Mohawks, who tomahawked and beheaded the missionaries. John de Brebeuf made two missionary journeys to the Hurons, in spite of many difficulties. (For instance, the Huron medicine men blamed the Jesuits for an epidemic of smallpox.) He composed catechisms and a dictionary of the Huron language, and eventually his efforts bore fruit; 7000 of the Hurons were converted. In 1649 he and St. Gabriel Lalemant were captured by the Iroquois, and tortured for four hours before dying.

LESSONS

1. Saints typically go "above and beyond" the call of duty. After enduring torture and other hardships, St. Isaac Jogues was certainly entitled to remain safe in his homeland of France, but he felt called to return to North America, even though he knew this might well mean martyrdom.

2. Sharing the Gospel effectively requires us to respect other people and their culture, even as we try to teach and assist them. St. John de Brebeuf took the time to learn the Huron language, and his efforts helped make it possible to share the Good News of salvation with the native Americans.

3. Jesus knew His followers wouldn't always be welcomed; nevertheless, Catholicism is a missionary religion by its very nature, and all believers must be willing to share their faith whenever possible.

October 20 — St. Paul of the Cross
(Priest and Founder)

St. Paul of the Cross (1694–1775) was an Italian mystic and the founder of the Passionist Order. Paul belonged to a large and devout middle-class family, and was the second of sixteen children; he worked for a time to help support his younger brothers and sisters, and then joined the army of Venice at age twenty. In 1720, however, Paul had a spiritual experience which convinced him that God desired him to found a missionary order which would focus on the Passion and Cross of Christ. Paul and one of his brothers, after being ordained as priests in Rome in

1727, established the Passionist Order. The first ten years were difficult, but Paul's fervent preaching attracted others, and gradually the Order grew. In order to bring inactive Catholics to a deeper commitment to Christ, Paul developed the concept of parish missions, which involved processions, street preaching, vigils, and penitential works. Paul's sermons, preaching with arms outstretched and a cross in hand, moved even the hardest hearts; one soldier told him, "Father, I have been in great battles without even flinching at the cannon's roar, but when I listen to you I tremble from head to foot." Paul's preaching was often challenging, but he dealt gently with penitents in the confessional, urging them to bear in whatever way possible their crosses in daily life. St. Paul died in Rome in 1775.

LESSONS

1. Large families have often been a plentiful source of religious vocations for the Church; as a "domestic church," the family plays a vital role in helping people respond to God's call.

2. In addition to evangelizing those who've never heard the Gospel, an important part of the Church's mission is reaching out to inactive or non-practicing Catholics and helping them renew their faith.

3. Sharing the Gospel often demands a balance between forceful challenges and gentle encouragement; St. Paul of the Cross combined these approaches as a preacher and a confessor.

October 23 — St. John of Capistrano (Priest)

The Italian priest St. John of Capistrano (1386–1456) was a well-educated lawyer; when only twenty-six, he became governor of the region of Perugia. Captured in a local war several years after this, John decided to change his life; he entered the Franciscan Order at the age of thirty, and was ordained a priest four years later. At that time the Church was experiencing a schism (a division between two different groups), and many people had grown lukewarm in the faith. The Franciscans themselves were divided over whether or not to remain true to the original ideals of St. Francis of Assisi. John and a dozen other Franciscans sought to renew the Church by their preaching and religious practices. They conducted missions throughout Europe; John himself preached with great success in many parts of Italy. Their efforts contributed to a spiritual renewal in the Church, and John's influence and legal background eventually led to the Franciscans' return to the ideals of their founder. Several popes chose John for various religious and diplomatic missions. He managed to achieve a reunion of the Greek and Armenian churches with Rome (though unfortunately, this proved to be temporary), and he preached a crusade against the Turks, who had captured Constantinople in 1453. John's presence on the battlefield encouraged the Hungarian general Hunyadi and his troops, and they won a great victory near the city of Belgrade. John soon afterward contracted the plague, and died in 1456.

Lessons from the Lives of the Saints

1. Early life experiences can prepare us for a later spiritual mission. St. John's legal background helped him as a preacher, and increased his influence in his efforts to renew the Franciscan Order.

2. There may be times when Christian nations must defend themselves by force (and the Church has recognized the possibility of a "just war"); St. John was involved in such a struggle (though not as a combatant). Nevertheless, the message of the Gospel is meant to include peace and reconciliation, and these are the values which Christians should strive to uphold whenever possible.

October 24 — St. Anthony Claret
(Bishop and Missionary)

St. Anthony Claret (1807–1870) was a Spanish missionary priest and bishop who became known as the "Spiritual Father of Cuba." The son of a weaver, he initially followed in his father's footsteps; while working in the textile mills of Barcelona, he studied Latin in preparation for the priesthood, and was ordained at the age of twenty-eight. Ill health prevented Anthony from becoming a Jesuit or Carthusian, so he devoted himself to giving missions and retreats throughout Spain, during which he emphasized the importance of the Eucharist and the beauty of devotion to the Immaculate Heart of Mary. Anthony and five other priests founded a religious order (the Claretians) to continue this ministry in Spain; in 1849 he himself, through the influence of Queen Isabella II, was appointed archbishop of the diocese of Santiago in Cuba. Anthony responded vigorously to the spiritual needs of his flock, and also gave religious instruction to blacks, stamped out concubinage, and promoted efforts to diversify the island's agriculture. Wealthy slaveholders and plantation owners reacted violently, and there were fourteen attempts on the bishop's life — one by a man who slashed Anthony's face and wrist. (Anthony arranged for the man's resulting death sentence to be commuted to a term in prison.) In 1857 Queen Isabella recalled Anthony and made him her court chaplain, to the saint's great reluctance; however, this allowed him the opportunity to promote a Catholic press in Spain (and he himself wrote over 200 books and pamphlets). When the royal family went into exile in 1868, Anthony accompanied the queen to France, and from there he went to the First Vatican Council in Rome, where he won the admiration of his fellow bishops. Anthony died soon afterward, and was canonized in 1950.

LESSONS

1. Many saints have humble beginnings, but these are often an asset; St. Anthony Claret's experience in the textile mills undoubtedly helped him sympathize with the slaves and poor workers of Cuba.

2. We can do much more for God by following His will rather than our own plans. Anthony's unfulfilled desire to be a Jesuit or Carthusian priest instead led to a successful preaching ministry, and his obedient acceptance of a position at court allowed him to do important work in Catholic publishing.

3. Even victims of violence are called to forgive others in Christ's Name (as St. Anthony did when he interceded for his attacker).

October 28 — Saints Simon and Jude (Apostles)

October 28 is the feast of the apostles Simon and Jude. Simon was known as the Zealot (Luke 6:15), for he was a member of the Zealot party (a Jewish movement dedicated to driving the Romans out of Palestine by force). Jesus' words must have, in some powerful way, touched Simon's heart, for this supporter of violence became an apostle of peace. Little is known of his later life; some accounts state that he preached first in Egypt, then in Persia, where he was martyred (perhaps with St. Jude). Jude (also known as Thaddeus) had the same name as Judas Iscariot; we refer to him as Jude to avoid confusing him with Jesus' betrayer. Jude and his brother James (also an apostle) are sometimes identified as cousins of Jesus; their true claim to fame, however, is not that they were related to Christ, but that they "heard the word of God and observed it" (Luke 11:27). One of the New Testament epistles is named after Jude (though most scholars believe he was probably not the author). Virtually nothing is known about St. Jude's later life; however, he has become known as the patron saint of lost causes.

LESSONS

1. God's peace is the only one which lasts. The Zealots failed in their efforts to liberate Palestine; St. Simon, by becoming a follower of Christ, helped bring spiritual freedom to many people.

2. Devotions to St. Jude as the patron saint of lost causes remind us never to give up hope, for — as Jesus said — "for God all things are possible" (Matthew 19:26).

November

November 1 — Feast of All Saints

The Feast of All Saints commemorates the lives of all the holy men and women of history who do not have specific feast days of their own — that is, the members of the "great multitude which no one could count" (Revelation 7:9) — only a small number of which can be included in the Church's liturgical calendar. The process by which the Church declares a person to be a saint is called canonization; when a person is canonized, this technically means that the Church is absolutely certain that he or she is indeed in Heaven (and thus, by definition, a living person can never be declared a saint). The canonization process is generally long and complicated, for the Church is determined that only those truly worthy of this honor be declared saints. Evidence and information about the candidate's life is carefully collected and examined, and a certifiable miracle, performed through the candidate's intercession, is required (for the ability to intercede with God is an important sign of the person's actual sanctity). If this point is reached, the person is beatified — that is, given the title "Blessed." After further examination and an additional miracle, the candidate is officially canonized by the Church — an event marked by special ceremonies and great rejoicing (especially in the home town or country of the new saint). The entire canonization process rarely lasts less than twenty years, and usually takes much longer. While canonization officially gives the title "Saint" to a person, in its simplest sense, being a saint means living in Heaven with God — a vocation or calling given to all of us.

LESSONS

1. Except for the Virgin Mary, all of the saints were — like us — sinners. Through the help of God's grace, they overcame their faults and achieved outstanding holiness — something we too are called to do. ·

2. Because intercessory prayer is pleasing to God (1 Timothy 2:3), the saints — who are now perfect in love — are eager to pray on our behalf, and because the prayer of a righteous person is very powerful (James 5:16), asking the saints to assist us can be spiritually beneficial and rewarding.

November 2 — Feast of All Souls

Just as the Feast of All Saints acknowledges the "Church triumphant" (the saints in Heaven), the Feast of All Souls acknowledges the "Church suffering" (the souls in purgatory — whom we might call "future saints").

As early as the second century Christians commemorated the anniversary of a believer's death — especially if that person had been a martyr — and in the seventh century St. Isidore of Seville, among others, promoted the observance of a single day for this purpose. Under the leadership of St. Odilo, abbot of the monastery of Cluny, the Benedictines in 998 assigned the Feast of All Souls to its current date of November 2, and by the fourteenth century this practice was observed throughout the Church. The Feast is closely connected to the Church's teaching on purgatory: "All who die in God's grace and friendship, but still imperfectly purified, are indeed assured of their eternal salvation but after death they undergo purification, so as to achieve the holiness necessary to enter the joy of heaven" (*Catechism of the Catholic Church*, no. 1030). This teaching is supported by a number of Scripture passages (2 Maccabees 12:43–46; Revelation 21:27; Matthew 18:24; Luke 12:58–59; and 1 Corinthians 3:12–15), and the Church further teaches that our prayers and sacrifices on behalf of the souls in purgatory can greatly aid them in this purification process.

LESSONS

1. Our moral decisions have an importance and effect far greater than commonly realized — and so we must make every effort to grow in grace here on earth and to repair the spiritual harm our sins have caused.

2. Because we are all a part of the Body of Christ (1 Corinthians 12:26–27), we have a moral obligation to show concern for those who suffer in purgatory by offering prayers and sacrifices on their behalf; as 2 Maccabees says, it is an "excellent and noble" thing to pray for the dead (12:43).

November 3 — St. Martin de Porres (Lay and Religious Brother)

The Dominican lay brother St. Martin de Porres (1579–1639) is considered the patron saint of interracial justice and harmony. Born in Lima, Peru, Martin was a mulatto, the illegitimate son of a Spanish landowner and a Negro or possibly Indian woman. It was eight years before Martin's father acknowledged him; later, after the birth of Martin's sister, the Spaniard abandoned his family. The resulting social stigma and poverty didn't embitter Martin; even as a child, he showed love and concern for everyone. At the age of twelve his mother apprenticed him to a barber-surgeon (the two professions were generally one and the same back then); several years later, after gaining experience helping the poor and sick, Martin applied to be a "lay helper" in the Dominican Order (feeling himself unworthy to be a religious brother). For nine years he worked with the poor and spent many hours in prayer and penance; then his community, impressed with his humility and charity, prevailed upon Martin to make full religious profession. Martin continued to nurse the sick; he also cared for slaves brought over from Africa, and helped found an orphanage. He was an effective fundraiser, obtaining money for the poor and to provide dowries for girls who would otherwise be unable to marry. Martin had the gift of bilocation (seeming to be in two places at once), and sometimes levitated during prayer; he worked miraculous cures, and had amazing control over animals (providing food to strays and caring for them at his sister's house). Through all of this, he remained a very simple and humble person.

LESSONS

1. All people are important in God's eyes, and have the potential for holiness — in spite of race, nationality, or social or economic class.

2. We can't control what happens to us, whether in childhood or later life, but we can choose whether we'll respond with bitterness or with patience and understanding.

November 4 — St. Charles Borromeo (Cardinal)

St. Charles Borromeo (1538–1584) played an important role in the Catholic Reformation. Born in Milan of noble parents, he desired from an early age to serve the Church. In 1559 his uncle, Cardinal de Medici, became Pope Pius IV, and appointed young Charles as cardinal and administrator of the archdiocese of Milan (even though Charles was still a layman). Charles took his duties seriously, implementing various reforms, and the Vatican entrusted him with several important duties. When his older brother died, Charles' parents insisted he marry, but instead he decided to become a priest, and was ordained at age twenty-five. He played a major role in bringing the Council of Trent to a successful conclusion; the Council, which was the Church's response to the Protestant Reformation, upheld Catholic teaching and decreed various reforms. Charles vigorously implemented these decrees within his own diocese, establishing "Sunday schools" for children and seminaries for the education of future priests. He also emphasized the importance of caring for the poor, and tried to restore a greater sense of reverence to the Mass. Charles lived simply, practiced severe penances, and gave large sums to the poor; during a plague in 1576 he personally attended to the ill and dying, and administered the city when the civil authorities fled. During his life St. Charles had many difficulties to overcome, including a speech impediment (which made it hard for him to preach), and opposition to his reforms (resulting, on one occasion, in an assassination attempt). His constant attention to the needs of his diocese caused his health to deteriorate rapidly, and he died in 1584 at the age of forty-six.

LESSONS

1. Young adults who take their faith seriously are capable of fulfilling important responsibilities and of doing great things in God's Name.

2. Living a life of service to others and to the Church can involve a heavy price (as in the case of preventing St. Charles from marrying, and later costing him his health), but this can be a path leading toward great happiness, holiness, and self-fulfillment.

November 10 — St. Leo the Great
(Pope and Doctor)

St. Leo I (d. 461), a Pope and Doctor (an eminent and reliable teacher) of the Church, is known to history as Leo the Great. Little or nothing is known of his early life, but after his election as Pope in 440, Leo played a major role in shaping the history of the Church and of Western Europe itself. The fifth century was a time of crisis both for the Church and for the remnants of the Roman Empire in Western Europe. The heresy of *Monophysitism* (which wrongly stated that Christ did not have both a human and divine nature) was rampant, but Leo's skillful use of the papacy's prestige helped uphold the Church's teaching. The Council of Chalcedon met in 451 to consider issues raised by the heresy. Pope Leo sent a doctrinal letter to the Council; the bishops received the letter respectfully (stating that "St. Peter speaks through Leo") and used it to reassert the Church's teaching that Jesus is both true God and true man. In addition to strengthening Rome's theological authority, Leo increased the secular, or worldly, authority of the Church. In 452, after government officials fled in fear, he went out to meet Attila the Hun and convinced the barbarian leader to spare the city of Rome and to withdraw after receiving a ransom. When the barbarian tribe known as the Vandals occupied Rome three years later, Leo prevented them from massacring the inhabitants (their normal practice). St. Leo was a gifted administrator, and also a great spiritual leader; his writings presented Christian teachings in very insightful but still easily-understood terms. He died in 461, and was declared a Doctor in 1754.

LESSONS

1. When heresy or false values are widespread in society or in the Church, witnessing to the truth is one of the most important services a Christian can render; just as the bishops used Pope Leo's teaching in upholding Church doctrine, there may be people of good will today waiting to do what's right — if we show the way by our leadership and example.

2. St. Leo increased the Church's prestige because he, unlike the local officials, did not abandon them during a time of danger; in the same way, our example of faith and commitment can give others a favorable impression of the Church.

November 11 — St. Martin of Tours (Bishop)

St. Martin of Tours (ca. 316–397) was born in modern-day Hungary and raised in Italy; at age fifteen he was inducted into the army against his will. Martin became a catechumen — one actively preparing for entry into the

Church. One winter day he saw a beggar shivering in the cold, so he drew his sword and cut his military cloak in two, keeping half for himself and giving the rest to the grateful beggar. That night Martin had a dream in which he saw Christ wearing the partial cloak he had given away; Jesus said, "Martin, still a catechumen, has covered Me with this garment." Martin was baptized soon after this, and after some difficulties, was allowed to leave the army. He became a monk, then was ordained a priest in 360; for ten years he lived and preached near Poitiers in France. About 370 Martin reluctantly became bishop of Tours (only by trickery did the people get him to come to the city so that they might elect him). Martin travelled widely as a missionary, reaching remote areas and gaining a reputation as a miracle worker; as a bishop, he strongly opposed heresy, and also opposed those in the Church who felt heretics should be put to death. Though he encountered opposition, Martin remained faithful until his death in 397. St. Martin of Tours is considered the founder of French monasticism, and was one of the first non-martyrs to be widely venerated as a saint.

LESSONS

1. "Whatever you do for the least of My brothers and sisters, you do for Me" (Matthew 25:40). St. Martin experienced this literally when he took pity upon a freezing beggar — and in this way he showed himself truly worthy of membership in Christ's Church.

2. Even though we might not desire a certain ministry, it may still be our calling from God; though reluctant to be a bishop, St. Martin accepted, and thereby gave great glory to the Lord.

November 12 — St. Josaphat (Bishop and Martyr)

The bishop and martyr St. Josaphat (1580–1623) dedicated his life to promoting the reunion of parts of the Orthodox Church with the Church of Rome. Born as John Kunsevich in what was then Poland, he became a Basilian monk and then a priest; Josaphat served as abbot of a monastery in the city of Vilna, and there gained a reputation as an effective preacher and an ascetic. Because of his holiness and reasonableness, Josaphat was appointed as Catholic bishop of Vitebsk, a city some 300 miles west of Moscow; it was hoped his diplomacy would disarm those Orthodox who violently opposed reunion with Rome. By careful instruction, reform of the clergy, and personal example, Josaphat managed to unite most of the Orthodox in Lithuania with the Roman Church, but serious difficulties remained. In 1623 dissidents established a rival clergy in Vitebsk, and efforts were made to scare off Bishop Josaphat. A priest was sent to shout insults at him from his own courtyard, but Josaphat had him brought inside and treated him kindly. At this, his opponents assembled in a mob and broke into the house. They released the priest and assaulted Josaphat, stabbing and shooting him. The saint's body was thrown into a river, but was later recovered and buried in Poland. St. Josaphat's last words were, "I am here among you as your shepherd and . . . I am ready to die for the holy union, for the supremacy of St. Peter and of his successor, the Supreme Pontiff."

LESSONS

1. Because of the intense feelings involved, religious unity is often very difficult to achieve or restore — yet all Christians are called to help fulfill Jesus' prayer that his followers be united (John 17:21).

2. Unity must be based on truth. Though a mild and reasonable man, St. Josaphat would not compromise on the supremacy and authority of the papacy.

November 13 — St. Frances Cabrini (Foundress)

The first American to be canonized, St. Frances Cabrini (1850–1917) was born in Italy, the youngest of thirteen children. She was trained as a school teacher, but desired to be a nun; twice she was rejected because of poor health. Undeterred, Frances became head of a small orphanage, and in 1877 made her vows there; when the orphanage closed three years later, she founded the Missionary Sisters of the Sacred Heart, and established several convents in Italy. Frances had long dreamt of serving as a missionary in China; when she sought permission from Pope Leo XIII, however, he said to her, "Do not go to the East, but to the West." In 1889 she and six of her sisters arrived in New York and began working among the many Italian immigrants in the city. Mother Cabrini encountered many difficulties: she had trouble learning English, she faced religious opposition, and she frequently had to return to Italy — which meant conquering her lifelong fear of traveling over water. Nonetheless, she persevered, and eventually met with great success; in thirty-five years, she founded no less than sixty-seven institutions to care for the poor, the sick, and the uneducated. Her level-headedness and fundraising skills won her much admiration and support, but she always placed her primary trust in God; to every difficulty in ministry, she responded: "Who is doing this? We — or the Lord?" Mother Cabrini became a naturalized citizen, and continued her work among the poor until her death in 1917.

LESSONS

1. Setbacks and disappointments often turn out to be part of God's plan for us. St. Frances Cabrini didn't become a nun as soon as she wanted, and she never fulfilled her dream of doing missionary work in China, but God had a very important mission for her in the United States.

2. Even saints have common problems (such as Mother Cabrini's hydrophobia, and her difficulty learning a new language); perseverance even in the face of such routine cases can lead to holiness.

3. As St. Frances Cabrini noted, we shouldn't be discouraged by difficulties in ministry — for everything ultimately depends on the Lord, not on us.

November 15 — St. Albert the Great (Bishop and Doctor)

The teacher of St. Thomas Aquinas, St. Albert the Great (1206–1280) was a German bishop and philosopher. Albert was the eldest son of a noble family. He studied at the University of Padua, and then — despite fierce family opposition — joined the newly-formed Order of Preachers (the Dominicans). Albert gained a Master's degree in theology at the University of Paris in 1244; after this, he served as director of studies at the University of Cologne, where Thomas Aquinas was one of his pupils. Albert attempted to understand the works of the Greek philosopher Aristotle, who was until then largely ignored by the Church; this helped develop a climate favorable for Aquinas' later efforts to synthesize Christian theology and Greek wisdom. In addition to instructing others, Albert was a great scholar in his own right, being interested in a wide range of subjects. He was known as "the Universal Teacher," and wrote on theology, biblical studies, logic, rhetoric, ethics, mathematics, physics, astronomy, chemistry, biology, geography, geology, and botany. In 1260 Albert was appointed bishop of the city of Regensburg, but after two years he resigned this office, feeling that he could contribute more to the Church as a teacher. Albert returned to the University of Cologne and taught there until his death in 1280. In 1931 he was declared a Doctor (an eminent and reliable teacher) of the Church.

LESSONS

1. Sometimes other Christians reap the harvest planted through our efforts (cf. John 4:37–38); St. Albert's scholarship paved the way for St. Thomas Aquinas' valuable synthesis of Aristotle's philosophy and Christian theology.

2. Albert was an expert in many fields, both religious and scientific; contrary to the modern myth that science and religion are opposed to each other, Albert knew that ultimately all truth is related.

3. True glory comes not from high rank or important positions, but from using our talents in accord with God's plan. St. Albert knew that, for him, it was more important to be a teacher than a bishop.

November 16 — St. Margaret of Scotland (Queen)

St. Margaret of Scotland (ca. 1045–1093) was a granddaughter of an English king, but was born in exile (probably in Hungary). She and her family were shipwrecked off the coast of Scotland, where they were given refuge by Malcolm III, the Scottish king. Malcolm became enchanted with young Margaret, and they were married in 1070. The king was a good but uncultured man; Margaret used her influence to soften his temper and to help him become holy. She herself was strong-willed and virtuous; as queen, her power was great, and she didn't hesitate to use it to promote church reforms, to raise the level of Scottish culture, and to improve the living conditions of the poor. Malcolm trusted his wife's judgment and often consulted her in affairs of state, and the royal couple founded several churches and monasteries. Margaret was a good mother, personally seeing to the religious education of her eight children. (Her son David became one of the most popular and holy Scottish kings, and through the marriage of her daughter Matilda to King Henry I of England, Margaret was an ancestress of the present British royal family.) Margaret was especially known for her concern for the poor; not only did she give large sums of money for their care, but she personally visited and nursed the sick, and washed the feet of the poor as a sign of Christian service. Margaret also set aside regular time for prayer, fasting, and reading

the Bible. In 1093 Malcolm and his oldest son were treach-
erously killed by foreign enemies; St. Margaret, already on
her death bed, died four days later.

LESSONS

1. As Jesus says, much will be expected of those to whom
much is given (Luke 12:48). As queen, St. Margaret had
great wealth and power — and she used these advantages
on behalf of the lowly.

2. No matter how powerful and important we are, one
of our most important responsibilities is helping our spouses
and children grow in holiness, as St. Margaret realized.

November 16 — St. Gertrude (Virgin and Mystic)

At the age of five, St. Gertrude (ca. 1256–1302) was taken
by her family to the convent of Helfta in central Germany,
where she was to spend the rest of her life. Gertrude and
her friend St. Mechtilde practiced a spirituality known as
nuptial mysticism, in which they came to see themselves as
brides of Christ. Gertrude received an excellent education
at the convent, but upon experiencing a vision of Christ
when she was twenty-five, she lost all interest in secular
studies, and instead devoted herself to studying the Bible,
the writings of the Church Fathers, and the Mass. Thus,
she was able to achieve an ideal spiritual balance: an intense
personal prayer life and a complete devotion to communal
worship in the liturgy. Gertrude received many spiritual
graces and revelations, some of which were later written
down and played a major role in medieval mysticism. St.

Gertrude is often called "the Great"; she died in 1302, and is considered one of the great mystics of the thirteenth century.

LESSONS

1. Certain female saints and mystics have become spiritual "brides of Christ"; the Book of Revelation describes the Church as Christ's Bride (21:2), and in this sense, all of us — as members of the Church — are called to a high degree of purity and fidelity.

2. Just as life involves a balance between solitude and interaction with others, so our spirituality should be balanced between personal prayer and communal worship.

November 17 — St. Elizabeth of Hungary (Princess)

St. Elizabeth (1207–1231), daughter of the King of Hungary, lived a short life, but became widely known for her humility and charity toward the poor. At the age of fourteen Princess Elizabeth was married to Ludwig IV of Thuringia. Though the marriage was arranged for political reasons, Ludwig and Elizabeth loved each other deeply; they had three children, and spent six happy years together in Wartburg Castle. During this time Elizabeth received spiritual direction from a Franciscan friar, and she devoted herself to a life of prayer, sacrifice, and care for the poor and sick. In 1227 Ludwig went to join the Crusades, but he soon died, and Elizabeth was grief stricken. (It was reported that, upon hearing of his death, she ran through the castle shrieking hysterically.) Instead of finding sympathy from her husband's family, Elizabeth found enmity; they regarded her charitable ventures as a squandering of the royal treasury. Elizabeth was mistreated and eventually driven out of the castle; according to legend, her brother-in-law forced her to leave in the dead of winter while she had a baby at her breast. When her husband's allies returned from the Crusades, however, Elizabeth's position was restored. She arranged to have her children provided for, and then, in 1228, joined the Third Order (for lay persons) of St. Francis. Elizabeth founded a hospital in honor of St. Francis, and spent the remaining years of her life there, caring for the sick. Her constant efforts on behalf of others taxed her health, and she died before her twenty-fourth birthday in 1231. St. Elizabeth's tremendous popularity resulted in her canonization four years later.

LESSONS

1. Like other people, saints are capable of experiencing great earthly happiness and intense sorrow; St. Elizabeth was deeply in love with her husband, and utterly devastated by his death. She achieved holiness by being willing to offer both these experiences wholeheartedly to God.

2. Christian ministry and efforts to bring about a better society must be nourished by prayer. St. Elizabeth labored tirelessly on behalf of the poor, but was careful to set aside time for her own prayers and spiritual devotions (without which her other efforts would have come to naught).

3. Even those born into a privileged position are called to treat everyone with dignity and respect.

November 18 — St. Rose Philippine Duchesne
(Virgin and Religious)

St. Rose Philippine Duchesne (1769–1852) was born in Grenoble, France, of a wealthy family. She was strong-willed and determined; at the age of nineteen, she entered the convent without her parents' knowledge, and remained there in spite of their opposition. When the convent was closed during the French Revolution, she began caring for the poor and the sick, opened a school for homeless children, and — at the risk of her life — secretly helped priests in hiding. When the political situation allowed, Rose Philippine and a few other nuns tried to reestablish their former convent, but failed, so they instead joined the newly-formed Society of the Sacred Heart (and St. Madeleine Sophie Barat, the young superior of the Order, became a lifelong friend). Rose Philippine soon became a supervisor of the novitiate (where new sisters were trained) and of a school, but her dream was to go to North America and work among the Indians there. At the age of forty-nine, she and eleven other sisters made the long and difficult journey to New Orleans and then to St. Louis, only to be told by the bishop that there was no place for them to live and work there. Instead, he sent them to what Rose Philippine sadly referred to as "the remotest village in the U.S.": St. Charles, Missouri. She tried to establish a school there, but failed due to cold and hunger, so she and the sisters set up several schools elsewhere in the state, all the while enduring harsh conditions. Finally, when Rose Philippine was seventy-two, a mission was established among the Potawatomi Indians at a mission in Kansas, and she was able to move there. Though she didn't learn their language, the Indians soon gave her a name: "Woman who prays always" (for they noted the hours she spent in kneeling in prayer). St. Rose Philippine Duchesne died in 1852 at the age of eighty-three.

LESSONS

1. Failure in a worldly sense is no impediment to holiness; St. Rose Philippine Duchesne failed several times in her endeavors, but because she persevered in her efforts to serve God, she was ultimately successful.

2. Many times our example speaks louder than the words we say. St. Rose Philippine Duchesne couldn't communicate with the Potawatomi, but they were greatly impressed by her prayerfulness.

November 22 — St. Cecilia (Virgin and Martyr)

Virtually nothing is known about St. Cecilia, other than the fact she founded a church in Rome in the second or third century, and after her death, was buried in a place of honor in the cemetery of St. Callistus. During and soon after her life, Cecilia was apparently regarded as a holy but otherwise unremarkable person; within several centuries, however, there were numerous legends concerning her (few of which had any basis in fact). By the year 545 she was referred to as St. Cecilia (the Church did not have a formal canonization process until much later), and a Passion of St. Cecilia, claiming to describe her life and martyrdom, was written (though it may very well have confused her with another Cecilia, who was also an early Christian martyr). St. Cecilia has traditionally been regarded as the patron of religious musicians.

LESSONS

1. Much of the good we do in this life will never be known to others; what matters is that it is known to God. We know little of St. Cecilia's life, but God knows everything about her, and He rewards her for her holiness.

2. Music plays a very important role in our liturgies, for it is a way of lifting our minds and hearts up to God. As the Second Vatican Council stated, "Liturgical action is given a more noble form when sacred rites are solemnized in song, with the assistance of sacred ministers and the active participation of the people" (*Constitution on the Liturgy*, no. 112).

November 23 — St. Clement I (Pope and Martyr)

St. Peter is considered the first Pope; he was succeeded by St. Linus, St. Cletus, and then — around 91 AD — by St. Clement, a Roman of Jewish heritage. Little is known about Clement's life, though he is famous for his Epistle to the Corinthians. Some Christians in the Greek city of Corinth rebelled against the Church leaders there, causing a serious division or schism. Clement, as Bishop of Rome, wrote a letter to the rebels in which he urged them to submit to lawful Church authority. The letter, which has been called "a model of pastoral solicitude and firm paternal admonition," was well received by the Corinthians; it was an important precedent because it was the first known intervention by the Bishop of Rome into the affairs of another Christian community. Clement is said to have been martyred in 101, though accounts of his death (supposedly

by being tied to an anchor and then tossed into the sea)
are of uncertain reliability.

LESSONS

1. The proper use of authority is an important ministry,
and can be a great blessing to the Church; St. Clement's
timely intervention helped the Christians of Corinth restore and maintain the unity for which Jesus had prayed
(John 17:20–21).

2. From the earliest days of the Church, the preemi-
nence of the Bishop of Rome has been recognized and respected; St. Peter and his successors are indeed the "rock"
upon which the Church is founded (Matthew 16:18).

3. As St. Clement realized, true spiritual growth requires us to center our lives around God's will; as he wrote
in the Letter to the Corinthians, lasting happiness "will
come about if by our faith our minds remain fixed on
God; if we aim at what is pleasing and acceptable to Him,
if we accomplish what is in harmony with His faultless
will and follow the path of truth, rejecting all injustice,
viciousness, covetousness, quarrels, malice, and deceit."

November 23 — St. Columban
(Abbot and Missionary)

St. Columban (ca. 543–615) was a famous Irish missionary. He was born in the province of Leinster and received
a solid education. As a young man, he lived as a hermit;
then, after years of prayer and solitude, he and twelve
companions went to France as missionaries, establishing a

number of monasteries which later became important religious and cultural centers. Columban and his companions were respected for their dedication and sincerity, but their insistence on Church discipline provoked opposition, and several times Columban had to defend himself by writing to the Pope. In 610 the missionary rebuked a local king for his immoral lifestyle; in response, an angered queen mother had him and the others put on a ship for Ireland, but the ship was forced back by a storm, giving Columban the chance to continue preaching elsewhere in Europe. Eventually Columban and his friends reached Switzerland, and then crossed the Alps into Italy. St. Columban established a monastery at Bobbio, and died there in 615.

LESSONS

1. Upholding the truth may make us enemies, but it will also bring us God's blessing; St. Columban was more concerned with defending the truth than with personal popularity.

2. Sometimes it may be necessary to defend our ministry from opposition by appealing to a higher authority; St. Columban didn't hesitate to seek the approval and support of the Pope when his methods were criticized.

3. We must always be aware of our spiritual heritage; St. Columban wrote, "It is a glorious privilege that God should grant man His eternal image and the likeness of His character. Man's likeness to God, if he preserves it, imparts high dignity."

November 23 — Blessed Miguel Pro
(Priest and Martyr)

Blessed Miguel Augustin Pro (1891–1927) was born in Mexico on January 13, 1891. He was a high-spirited and mischievous child — characteristics which stood him in good stead during his brief but heroic priestly ministry. As a young man, he joined the Jesuits, and studied in the United States, Spain, and Belgium. He was ordained a priest in 1926, and later that year secretly arrived at Veracruz in Mexico. The Church there was suffering greatly as a result of the Mexican Revolution. President Plutaro Calles led a campaign for "Land and Liberty," but this soon degenerated into anti-Catholicism, in which the Church was blamed for the country's problems. Catholicism was outlawed, and a secret, or underground, Church developed. Fr. Pro went to Mexico City, where he delighted in wearing disguises and in remaining undetected by the police, all the while risking arrest. Under the cover of "dinner parties" and family gatherings, he performed secret Masses, baptisms, and confessions in private homes; there were many police spies, but also many faithful Catholics willing to assist him. When finally caught by the authorities, Fr. Pro was accused of involvement in a murder plot against government officials. Though he claimed innocence and there was no evidence against him, President Calles decided to make an example of him, and personally ordered his execution. Fr. Pro was taken to the police firing range on November 23, 1927; his final request was for a moment to pray. He knelt in prayer, then stood and held out his arms in the form of a cross. As the firing squad took aim, the priest said softly, *"Viva Cristo Rey"* ("Long

live Christ the King"). Mexican Catholics instantly venerated the martyred priest as a saint, and photographs of his
execution were treasured as holy cards. Fr. Miguel Pro was
beatified (declared Blessed) in 1988.

LESSONS

1. Jesus told His followers to be "clever as serpents and
innocent as doves" (Matthew 10:16), and there are times
when successful ministry requires this sort of shrewdness;
by his use of disguises, Blessed Miguel Pro accomplished
much good during his short priestly ministry.

2. Being a true follower of Christ doesn't depend on
the number of years of our ministry, but on our degree of
commitment; Fr. Pro served as a priest for little more than
a year, but in this short time achieved a degree of holiness
that will be honored for all eternity.

November 24 — St. Andrew Dung-Lac and Companions (Martyrs)

St. Andrew Dung-Lac was a Vietnamese priest; he and
his companions gave their lives for Christ. From the seven-
teenth century up until 1866, many Vietnamese Catholics
suffered extreme persecution, especially during the reign of
the Emperor Mihn-Mang (1820–1840). Today's feast honors
the martyrs of Vietnam, including ninety-six Vietnamese
clergy and lay persons, eleven Dominican missionaries from
Spain, and ten French missionaries belonging to the Paris
Foreign Mission Society. Numbered among the martyrs
were eight Spanish and French bishops, fifty priests (in-

cluding St. Andrew Dung-Lac and thirty-six others from Vietnam), and fifty-nine lay persons. These martyrs were canonized by Pope John Paul II on June 19, 1988.

LESSONS

1. Christian missionaries bring the Good News of salvation to peoples who would otherwise not be able to hear it, but this does not mean it's always welcome; as Jesus warned, "If the world hates you, realize that it hated Me first. If you belonged to the world, the world would love its own; but because you do not belong to the world . . . the world hates you" (John 15:18–19).

2. People of many different nationalities and backgrounds are able to work together and to experience unity through Jesus; European missionaries and Vietnamese clergy and laity are forever united in the glory of Christ's Kingdom because of their willingness to suffer and die for His Name.

November 30 — St. Andrew (Apostle and Martyr)

St. Andrew was the brother of St. Peter (Mark 1:16) and one of the Twelve Apostles. He and his brother were fishermen from the town of Bethsaida in Galilee. According to St. John's Gospel, Andrew became a follower of John the Baptist, who later pointed to Jesus and said, "Behold the Lamb of God" (John 1:35–42). Becoming convinced that Jesus was the Messiah, or long-promised Savior, Andrew sought out Peter and brought him to Christ. It was Andrew who, prior to Jesus' multiplication of the loaves and fish, pointed out the boy who had the only source of food for the crowd (John 6.8), and it was he who, with Philip, presented some of the Gentiles to Christ (John 12:22). Aside from these incidents, there is little mention of him in the Gospels, and virtually nothing else is known with certainty about his life. According to legend, St. Andrew preached in Bithynia, Scythia, Macedonia, and Achaia (southern Greece), where he was reportedly crucified on an X-shaped cross.

LESSONS

1. St. Peter was known for his outspoken, impetuous nature; we might reasonably assume that St. Andrew was the quieter of the two brothers. This did not detract from his ministry, however, for God is able to use people of all different personalities to further the coming of His Kingdom.

2. Bringing people to Jesus is one of the greatest things we can do; St. Andrew did this first for his brother, and later for some of the Gentiles seeking to meet Christ.

December

December 3 — St. Francis Xavier
(Priest and Missionary)

The famous Jesuit missionary St. Francis Xavier (1506–1552) was born in Spain; his intelligence and hard work allowed him to become a student, and eventually an instructor, at the prestigious University of Paris. While there he became a friend of St. Ignatius of Loyola, the founder of the Society of Jesus (the religious order known as the Jesuits). Ignatius tried to share his spiritual dreams and desires with Francis, but for a long time young Francis was more concerned with his promising academic career. Finally Ignatius repeated the words of Christ: "What profit does a man show if he gains the whole world, but loses his soul?" (Mark 8:36). Francis was convinced; he followed Ignatius' spiritual direction, and in 1534 became one of the original seven Jesuits. Francis was ordained a priest in 1537; several years later he and two companions sailed from Portugal on a missionary journey to India. Francis spent seven years laboring among the poor, and stated that the sufferings of the natives inflicted a "permanent bruise" on his soul. He wrote outspoken letters of complaint to the King of Portugal; in addition to working for an improvement of the natives' living conditions, Francis also tended their spiritual needs, personally baptizing thousands of people. After a year ministering in Malaysia, Francis went to Japan in 1549. Because he was officially a representative of the

King of Portugal, Francis was welcomed by the Japanese rulers and given permission to teach. After two years he left his small but growing community of converts in the care of a Portuguese priest, returned to India, and prepared for a trip to the forbidden land of China. Preaching the Gospel in China had long been Francis' dream, and in 1552 he arranged for a Portuguese ship to take him to the Chinese coast, where he would meet a Chinese captain who had agreed to smuggle him ashore. However, he became ill on the journey, and the Portuguese, fearing discovery, put him ashore on a small island. There Francis spent his last two weeks in a primitive hut, praying continuously until he died, with only a faithful companion to tend to him.

LESSONS

1. Not all saints respond quickly to God's call; it took time for St. Ignatius to persuade his young friend to join him. We too must continue being a good influence on others, even if it seems unsuccessful at first.

2. Not even saints are exempt from great disappointments; St. Francis Xavier died while relatively young, only a short distance from the land where he had long desired to preach the Gospel.

December 4 — St. John Damascene
(Monk and Theologian)

St. John Damascene (ca. 674–749) was born in Damascus in Syria, which was then under Moslem control. The Moslem rulers required Christians and Jews to pay a special tax if they wished to practice their religion; other than that, they were well-treated; in fact, many non-Moslems rose to positions of great economic or political importance. This was true of John's father, who held the office of royal treasurer. John was baptized as an infant; his tutor was a monk whom the Arabs had captured in Sicily and who was purchased from slavery by John's father. The monk gave John a solid education, particularly in theology; he also taught John's adopted brother Cosmas. As a young man John succeeded his father as royal treasurer. Though he lived in a Moslem court, John was able to practice a Christian lifestyle, and soon became known for his humility and virtue. After a number of years John resigned his position as treasurer, and he and his adopted brother Cosmas went to live as monks at the monastery of St. Sabas near Jerusalem. During this period a series of emperors in Constantinople attacked the use of icons, or religious images, which represented Christ and the saints. John wrote in defense of this practice, angering the emperors (but because he lived in a Moslem land, he was beyond their reach). John and Cosmas spent much of their time writing books and religious hymns. Cosmas (who was later declared a saint himself) was made a bishop, a role which he fulfilled admirably; John remained at the monastery of St. Sabas for the rest of his life, writing books of theology and poetry. He died about the year 749; in 1890 he was declared a Doctor (an eminent and reliable teacher) of the Church.

LESSONS

1. Sometimes, as with St. John Damascene, saints are formed in non-Christian lands. This is a message of hope

for present-day Americans (for many believe ours is now a "post-Christian" society).

2. Important worldly positions can be a prelude to a life of serving God; though in charge of the royal treasury, St. John decided to seek after heavenly treasure instead.

3. Religious art — including icons and hymns — can be a valid and important aid to spiritual growth.

December 6 — St. Nicholas (Bishop)

Little factual information is available about St. Nicholas, though there are many legends regarding him. He lived in the fourth century, and died about the year 350. Nicholas was bishop of Myra, a city in Asia Minor (modern-day Turkey). The most famous story about him involves three sisters who feared they would never marry, as their father was too poor to provide a dowry. Nicholas is said to have secretly tossed a bag of coins through a window in their house on three separate occasions, thus making it possible for them to find husbands. Another story credits him with miraculously multiplying grain from an imperial grainship that stopped at Myra on the way to Rome, thereby providing food for the people during a famine. St. Nicholas is honored throughout the Christian world; he is the patron saint of sailors, children, merchants, and even pawnbrokers. As the patron of children, Nicholas is the source of "Father Christmas" — the religious precursor of Santa Claus (and the name "Santa Claus" is itself a variation of the saint's name). In some countries the custom continues of giving presents on his feast day; in one popular variation, each person receives either a gift of candy or a lump of coal that night (depending on his or her behavior).

LESSONS

1. St. Nicholas is the saint most associated with giving presents, and gift-giving is at the heart of Christian faith: "God so loved the world that He gave His only Son" (John 3:16).

2. According to legend, Bishop Nicholas preferred to give his gifts in secret. In the same way, if we truly desire to help others in Christ's Name, it's not important that our efforts be made known or that we receive credit for them. Instead, our Father Who sees what is hidden will repay us (cf. Matthew 6:18).

December 7 — St. Ambrose (Bishop and Doctor)

St. Ambrose (340–397) was a great bishop and scholar of the fourth century. The son of a Roman official in Gaul (France), he received a classical education; after practicing law in Roman courts, he was appointed governor of northern Italy. When the bishop of Milan died in 374, Ambrose was chosen to replace him by public acclamation, even though he was only a catechumen and not yet baptized. The new bishop faced many challenges: he had to cope with imperial interference in religion, efforts to restore paganism, and the heresy of Arianism, which had important support in high places. In each case he responded courageously and effectively. When, in 390, the emperor had several thousand citizens of Greece executed for causing a riot, Ambrose publicly condemned him and demanded he do penance — and the emperor submitted. Though he could be fierce and uncompromising with the powerful, Ambrose showed great kindness to the lowly; his first act upon being elected bishop was to give away almost all his personal property to the poor. He lived frugally, and organized charities for the needy; on one occasion he had gold vessels from the altar melted down and sold to provide money for ransoming some Catholics captured by barbarians. The bishop was active in catechizing pagans, his most famous convert being St. Augustine. As a teacher and author, Ambrose freely adapted pagan literature and philosophy to the teaching of Christianity; he also helped make hymns a popular means of praising God and promoting true doctrine. St. Ambrose died in Milan in 397.

LESSONS

1. God's law is higher than human law, and no one is exempt from it; as St. Ambrose said, "The emperor is in the Church; he is not above it."

2. There are times when secular or worldly ideas and images can legitimately be used to express Christian teachings. This can make it easier for others to accept the Gospel; it was St. Ambrose's use of pagan philosophy which helped attract St. Augustine to Christianity.

December 9 — Blessed Juan Diego (Layman)

A poor Indian near Mexico City named Cuatitlatoatzin was baptized and given the name Juan Diego. On Saturday December 9, 1531, Juan Diego — a fifty-seven-year-old widower — was walking past Tepeyac Hill when he saw a beautiful Native American maiden dressed like an Aztec (Mexican) princess. She sent him to the bishop of Mexico with the request that a shrine be built on the site. The bishop asked for a sign that he had truly seen the Virgin Mary. When Juan again saw her on December 12, she promised that his uncle — who was near death — would recover from his illness; she also told Juan to gather a bouquet of roses and present them to the bishop. (This would be a sign for him, because roses did not bloom in the middle of winter.) Juan gathered up the roses and carried them in his tilma (cloak); when he presented them by opening his tilma and letting the roses fall to the floor, the bishop stared at the tilma itself in amazement. Imprinted on the rough cactus-fiber was a beautiful portrait of the Mother of God, just as Juan had described her. Convinced of the authenticity of Juan's visions, the bishop had a small chapel built, and thousands of Indians and Spaniards flocked to the site. Juan Diego served as sacristan of the shrine until his death in 1548, and in the ten years following the apparition of Our Lady of Guadalupe, some eight million native Mexicans were baptized.

LESSONS

1. God is conscious of human limitations and cultural conditioning. Knowing that few Mexican Indians were accepting Catholicism because it seemed to be an outside religion imposed by foreigners, He sent the Virgin Mary to appear in a way that communicated to their culture — and they responded enthusiastically.

2. The Lord's power far transcends human understanding. To this day, scientists are unable to explain the pro-

cess by which the image of Mary was transferred to Juan Diego's tilma, and the most rigorous examinations have failed to cast doubts upon its authenticity.

December 11 — St. Damasus I (Pope)

St. Damasus I (ca. 305–384) was an important fourth century Pope. He was the son of a Roman priest (it was only centuries later that the Church required celibacy of the clergy), and became a deacon in his father's church. Later Damasus served as a secretary to Pope Liberius; when Liberius was banished by the emperor for refusing to submit to the heresy of Arianism, Damasus briefly followed him into exile. Upon Liberius' death in 366, Damasus was elected Bishop of Rome (Pope), though another deacon, Ursinus, was invalidly elected and consecrated at the same time by a minority of bishops. The civil government intervened in Damasus' behalf, but throughout his pontificate Ursinus' supporters continued to oppose him (and at one point even accused the elderly Damasus of unlikely crimes, such as adultery, against which he had to defend himself in court). In addition to opposing the antipope Ursinus, Damasus also had to struggle against various heresies and Church controversies. It was during his reign, however, that Christianity was declared the official religion of the Empire. Damasus is best known for encouraging his brilliant but temperamental secretary, St. Jerome, to translate the Bible into Latin (the common language); this work became known as the Vulgate, and remained the Church's official translation for centuries. Pope Damasus had a great appreciation of Church history; he drew up an official list of all the popes who preceded him, and had biographies written of the many Roman martyrs, while transforming their tombs into religious shrines. St. Damasus died in 384; St. Jerome described him as "an incomparable person, learned in the Scriptures, a virgin doctor of the virgin Church, who loved chastity and heard its praises with pleasure."

LESSONS

1. Because the Church exists in the world, it is not exempt from worldly controversies and divisions; however, God is able to use these unfortunate events to bring forth great leaders and saints.

2. As St. Damasus recognized, Church history can be an important way of discovering and preserving important truths about Christ's continuing presence and activity in the world.

3. Encouraging scholarship can be an important way of spreading the Gospel and encouraging faith.

December 13 — St. Lucy (Virgin and Martyr)

The virgin and martyr St. Lucy lived in Sicily at the end of the third century; very little is known about her with certainty. Christianity had not yet been legalized by the Roman Empire, and Christians were still subject to severe penalties during times of persecution. Lucy's vow of virginity made little sense to the pagans of Sicily; they viewed Christianity as nonsense and Lucy's adherence to it as complete foolishness. Early in the fourth century the Emperor Diocletian decreed a widespread persecution of Christianity, and it was during this persecution that Lucy was martyred. She was put to death in the Sicilian city of Syracuse in 304, supposedly after being denounced by a disappointed suitor. Nothing else is known of her, though there are a number of unlikely legends regarding her life. Lucy's memory was venerated at an early date, and her name was included in the canon (eucharistic prayer) of the Roman Mass (the source of our current Eucharistic Prayer I). Because her name is derived from the Latin word for light, St. Lucy's intercession is frequently sought by those suffering from diseases of the eye.

LESSONS

1. It's fitting that St. Lucy is considered a patroness of those suffering from eye problems, for she was able to see clearly in a spiritual sense; unlike most of her contemporaries, Lucy recognized the truth of Christianity and the value of virginity. Even today, we as Christians are called to recognize and proclaim truths that society seems unwilling to recognize or accept.

2. Though a young woman, St. Lucy met death courageously, proving that God's grace is sufficient to help us do whatever we must in order to remain faithful to Him.

December 14 — St. John of the Cross (Priest and Doctor)

Juan de Yepes, the Spanish mystic and poet known as St. John of the Cross (1542–1591), was ordained a Carmelite priest at the age of twenty-five. He met St. Teresa of Avila [October 15], who was dedicated to restoring the Carmelite

nuns to a holy and simple lifestyle. Moved by her example, John joined a reformed Carmelite monastery for men
and worked vigorously to promote the reforms. However,
his efforts led to great opposition; in 1577 the Carmelite
prior general ordered him imprisoned. John was kept in a
cramped, dark cell for nine months and treated brutally;
during this time he had mystical experiences and began developing a certain spiritual expertise, which he expressed
in his writings and in his poetry. After escaping, John held
various offices among the reformed friars, but was again
involved in controversy, once more suffering brutal treatment. He continued to write until his death in 1591, at the
age of forty-nine. His best known writings are *The Dark
Night of the Soul* and *The Ascent of Mt. Carmel*, which express the idea that suffering and joy are often united, and
that God is found most fully through self-surrender and
abandonment. St. John of the Cross was canonized in 1726,
and 200 years later was declared a Doctor (an eminent and
reliable teacher) of the Church.

LESSONS

1. If we choose, our misfortunes can be a source of great
spiritual growth; St. John would never have been able to
write so wonderfully on the spiritual life were it not for
his own sufferings.

2. Holiness and simplicity can be very threatening to
others (even including some members of the Church), but
if we persevere in our efforts to grow in grace, God will
bless us greatly.

3. Reform is an ongoing need in the Church — both of
religious institutions and in the lives of individual believers;

our efforts to overcome sin and to grow spiritually must
be ongoing and sincere.

December 21 — St. Peter Canisius
(Priest and Doctor)

St. Peter Canisius (1521–1597) was a Jesuit priest who
played a vital role in the Catholic Reformation of the sixteenth century. Peter was the son of the mayor of Nijmegen
in Holland; a studious young man, he obtained a master's
degree from the University of Cologne at age nineteen. It
had been Peter's intention to study law, but he happened to
meet Peter Faber, one of the first followers of St. Ignatius
of Loyola (the founder of the Jesuits). Young Peter was so
influenced that he himself entered the Society of Jesus in
1543. After his ordination three years later, Peter became
widely known for his scholarship, particularly his writings
on the works of St. Cyril of Alexandria and St. Leo the
Great. Peter was also a man of action. He took part in
the Council of Trent, taught at the first Jesuit school in
Messina, and reformed a Bavarian university, all the while
making time to visit the sick and the imprisoned. However,
Peter was best known for his preaching; he proclaimed the
Gospel in a way that touched the hearts of his listeners.
He was sent as provincial superior of the Jesuits to Vienna
and then southern Germany, where he labored vigorously
to defend and renew Catholicism following the Protestant
Reformation. Peter established schools, colleges, and seminaries, while also preaching and giving missions (it was
calculated that in a thirty year period, he travelled 20,000
miles on foot or by horse for this purpose). On being asked
if he felt overworked, he said, "If you have too much to

do, with God's help you will find time to do it all." Peter
was crippled by an illness at age seventy, but with the help
of a secretary, he continued to write and preach until his
death six years later. St. Peter Canisius, more than any
other person, is credited with keeping southern Germany
solidly Catholic.

LESSONS

1. It is not enough to know and believe that Catholicism is the True Faith established by Christ; there are also
times, as St. Peter Canisius knew, when it must be vigorously defended.

2. Many of us feel overworked — but as long as we're
ultimately trying to do everything for God's glory, and not
our own, the Lord will help us accomplish everything we
truly need to do.

December 23 — St. John of Kanty (Priest)

The Polish priest St. John of Kanty (1390–1473), also
known as St. John Cantius, was born near Oswiecim (a
town which, over 500 years later, would receive the infa-
mous name Auschwitz). John was a brilliant student at the
University of Krakow; after ordination to the priesthood,
he became a professor of theology. John's academic success
caused jealousy among some of his colleagues, and they
arranged for him to be sent away as pastor of a humble
parish. In spite of many difficulties, John did his best there,
and eventually he won the hearts of his parishioners. Some
time after this he returned to Krakow and there taught Sacred Scripture for the rest of his life. St. John was widely

known for his humility and especially for his kindness to the poor. He kept only what he absolutely needed to live on, and gave everything else away. It is said that on one occasion he was stopped by robbers, who took all his money and asked if he had any more. When John said he didn't, they left, but then he discovered some coins sewn in his cloak. John ran after the robbers, caught up with them, and gave them the coins. They were so amazed that they returned everything they had taken from him. During his lifetime, John made four pilgrimages to Rome — carrying his luggage on his back. He slept on a floor and ate sparingly; when urged to take better care of himself, he responded that the desert hermits of early Christianity, in spite of their austerity, lived long lives. John himself lived to the age of eighty-three; he died on Christmas Eve, 1473, and was canonized in 1767.

LESSONS

1. Even when we suffer from the jealousy of others, God continues to give us opportunities to serve Him and to grow in His grace.

2. Honesty and humility are always rewarded — sometimes in this life (as happened when John caught up with the men who robbed him), and certainly in the life to come.

December 26 — St. Stephen (Proto-Martyr)

St. Stephen was the first Christian martyr; all of our knowledge of him comes from chapters 6–7 of the Acts of the Apostles. Stephen was an early Jewish convert to

Christianity; he was one of the first seven deacons chosen to look after the needs of Greek-speaking widows, thereby freeing the apostles for the ministry of preaching. Stephen is described as a man "filled with faith and the Holy Spirit," and his ministry soon included preaching as well as caring for the poor. He worked wonders and made an impression on the people, and engaged various Jews in debates. They were no match for Stephen's eloquence and wisdom, and in their anger they arranged for him to be arrested on the charge of blasphemy. During his trial Stephen described a vision of Christ standing at God's right hand, enraging his hearers so much that they dragged him outside the gates of the city and inflicted on him the customary Jewish penalty of death by stoning. Stephen's last words were "Lord Jesus, receive my spirit . . . do not lay this sin against them." Stephen's murder, which would have occurred about the year 35 or 36, was witnessed and approved of by Saul of Tarsus, the future St. Paul. St. Stephen's courage did much to inspire the early Church, and his noble martyrdom may have begun to prepare Saul for his conversion which would soon occur on the road to Damascus.

LESSONS

1. God has a way of sometimes expanding our "job descriptions." Stephen was chosen to distribute food to the poor, but his ministry soon changed and grew dramatically. In the same way, God's plan for us might involve far more than we first expect.

2. Stephen's final words echoed those of Christ: he interceded on behalf of his executioners. Jesus also says to

us, "Love your enemies, and pray for those who persecute you" (Matthew 5:44).

3. Just as Stephen's courage in dying helped the early Christians realize that Christ would help them even in times of persecution, so our faith example can encourage others to remain firm.

December 27 — St. John (Apostle and Evangelist)

St. John and his brother St. James were sons of a Galilean fisherman named Zebedee; St. Peter and his brother St. Andrew were Galilean fishermen as well. John and James were one day mending their nets on the seashore when Jesus appeared and called them to follow him; this they did immediately, leaving behind their father with their nets and boat (Mark 1:19–20). This action was in character for the two brothers, for it seems they had an impetuous nature: once they arranged for their mother to intercede on their behalf (Mark 10:35–40), and on another occasion they urged Jesus to call down fire from Heaven to destroy an inhospitable Samaritan village (Luke 9:51–56) — an attitude which suggests why Jesus nicknamed them the "sons of thunder." John, along with his brother James and also with Peter, constituted a special group within the twelve apostles. They shared a very close friendship with Jesus and, alone of all the apostles, were present at the Transfiguration, at the raising of Jairus' daughter, and at Jesus' agony in the Garden of Gethsemane. St. John is often portrayed as a sensitive young man, one who shared a special intimacy with Christ. The Fourth Gospel, attributed to St. John, refers to him as "the disciple whom Jesus loved" (John 19:26).

LESSONS

1. Jesus, during His lifetime on earth, needed and desired close friendships; even now, as the Exalted Lord of all creation, He desires an intimate experience of friendship — with each one of us.

2. At first John's faith was immature, but he later came to understand Jesus better than any of the other disciples. We too are called to continue growing in faith, in spite of initial setbacks or failures.

3. Our Lord entrusted His Mother to the beloved disciple (John 19:26–27) — and because John herein symbolizes every Christian, Jesus is inviting all of us to experience a special relationship with Mary.

December 28 — Holy Innocents (Martyrs)

The Holy Innocents were the male infants killed near Bethlehem under the orders of King Herod the Great. St. Matthew's Gospel (2:1–3, 16–18) tells us that Herod, when informed by the magi and by his court astrologers of the birth of one who was destined to rule Israel, viewed the newborn child as a rival. The king thereupon ordered the murder of all the young male children living near Bethlehem in order to eliminate the imagined threat posed by the infant Jesus. Mary and Joseph, as St. Matthew tells us, fled with Jesus to Egypt in response to an angel's warning, thus thwarting Herod's evil scheme. The other male children under two years of age, however, were all found and put to death. The Holy Innocents thus became the first martyrs to die for Christ. (Some scholars believe that no more than twenty children were murdered, while one alleged private revelation puts the number of martyred children at thirty-eight, including six girls killed by mistake.) Veneration of the Holy Innocents as martyrs began at an early date, and it is the custom of Christian children in Bethlehem to gather in the Church of the Nativity and sing a hymn in their memory.

LESSONS

1. One of the Psalms praises God by stating, "Out of the mouths of babes and sucklings You have fashioned praise because of Your foes, to silence the hostile and the vengeful" (Psalm 8:3). Though they were unable to speak, the holy infants of Bethlehem bore witness to Christ by the shedding of their blood — and now they praise God forever in the glory of Heaven.

2. Because of his lengthy rule and magnificent building projects, King Herod is known to history as "Herod the Great" — yet his reign ended in abject failure. Conversely, the Holy Innocents — who lived only briefly in this world — have become truly great to those who see with eyes of faith.

3. Just as "Rachel wept for her children" (Matthew 2:18), so we are called to mourn the Holy Innocents of our own day — all the while working to save additional unborn lives from being ended by abortion.

December 29 — St. Thomas Becket
(Bishop and Martyr)

St. Thomas Becket (1118–1170) was born of a well-to-do English family; after receiving a good education, he was ordained a deacon in 1154. Becket was a close friend of King Henry II, and in 1155 the king chose him to serve as his royal chancellor. For seven years Becket served the king faithfully and well as a soldier, diplomat, and statesman. When the archbishop of Canterbury died in 1162, Henry decided to appoint his friend to the post (apparently hoping to gain influence over the Church in England). Thomas was ordained a priest the day before his installation as archbishop. Until then he hadn't been known as an especially holy man, but he suddenly underwent a spiritual renewal and adopted a prayerful and austere lifestyle; his new responsibilities transformed Thomas from a man of the world to a shepherd of souls. The discovery that Thomas placed his religious duties above his friendship with the king did not please Henry. Several controversies arose regarding conflicting claims of authority between Church and State; when Thomas upheld the Church's position, Henry felt his friend had betrayed him, and the archbishop was forced into exile in France for six years. In 1170 King Henry visited Thomas in France and was apparently reconciled with him; when Thomas returned to England, however, the quarrel was reignited by his efforts to discipline those bishops who had usurped his authority as archbishop. Upon hearing of this, Henry, who was still in France, cried out in rage, "Will no one rid me of this troublesome priest?" Four of his knights, hoping to win their master's favor, returned to England and, on the night of December 29, killed

Thomas in a side chapel of the cathedral in Canterbury. Europe was outraged by his murder, and three years later Thomas Becket was canonized by the pope; King Henry himself did public penance at the site of his murder.

LESSONS

1. God's grace works in unexpected ways; upon being installed as archbishop of Canterbury, a worldly Thomas Becket began fulfilling his new duties in a conscientious and dedicated manner.

2. Conflicts between Church and State are frequent in history, and perhaps even inevitable; Jesus warned His followers they would be hated and persecuted for not belonging to this world (John 15:18–21).

December 31 — St. Sylvester (Pope)

The fourth century Pope St. Sylvester was the thirty-third Bishop of Rome and the first to be elected after the legalization of Christianity. The great Roman Emperor Constantine was convinced that his victory over his rivals for the throne at the Battle of Milvian Bridge outside Rome was due to the intervention of Christ; in gratitude, he issued the Edict of Milan in 313, which allowed Christians to practice their faith freely without fear of persecution. Upon the death of Pope St. Miltiades the following year, Sylvester was elected to the throne of Peter. Emperor Constantine, a fervent convert to Christianity (though he was not baptized until just before his death some years later), often interfered in the affairs of the Church in a paternal way. Sylvester had to achieve a difficult balance between gratitude to the Emperor and maintaining the Church's independence; in this, he was fairly successful. St. Sylvester strove to preserve the Church's authority in religious matters; he presided over the ordinations of various priests, deacons, and bishops, and sent delegates to the Council of Nicea in 325 (which officially defined the Church's teaching that Jesus is both truly human and truly divine). St. Sylvester died in 335, and was one of the first non-martyrs to be venerated as a saint in Rome.

LESSONS

1. Followers of Christ have to contend not only with enemies, but sometimes also with well-meaning but overbearing friends; this requires a mixture of gentleness and firmness, as St. Sylvester demonstrated with the Emperor Constantine.

2. Jesus is the Lord of History, and just as He once made use of a Pharisee named Saul of Tarsus, and later a pagan Roman Emperor named Constantine, to advance the spread of the Gospel, so He will continue to work on the Church's behalf in our world today.

Bibliography

Butler's Lives of the Saints (Concise Edition), edited by Michael Walsh (Harper & Row, 1985).

In His Likeness, Rev. Charles Yost (Priests of the Sacred Heart, 1988).

Lives of the Saints for Every Day of the Year, Rev. Hugo Hoever (Catholic Book Publishing Co., 1993). Two volumes.

Saint of the Day, Leonard Foley O.F.M. (St. Anthony Messenger Press, 1990).

Saint-Watching, Phyllis McGinley (Thomas More Press, 1969).

The Avenel Dictionary of the Saints, Donald Attwater (Avenel Books, 1965).

About the Author

Rev. Joseph M. Esper is a priest of the Archdiocese of Detroit, and has written several books, including *After the Darkness* (a Catholic novel on the Coming of the Antichrist and the End of the World). He has also had articles published in *Fidelity*, *The Priest, Homiletic & Pastoral Review, Signs & Wonders for Our Times*, and *This Rock*.

Name Index

John Bosco (Priest and Founder), Jan. 31
John Chrysostom (Bishop and Doctor), Sept. 13
John Damascene (Monk and Theologian), Dec. 4
John Eudes (Priest and Founder), Aug. 19
John Fisher (Bishop and Martyr) and Thomas More (Martyr),
    June 22
John I (Pope and Martyr), May 18
John of Kanty (Priest), Dec. 23
John Leonardi (Priest and Founder), Oct. 9
John Neumann (Bishop), Jan. 5
John Vianney (Priest), Aug. 4
John of Capistrano (Priest), Oct. 23
John of God (Religious), Mar. 8
John of the Cross (Priest and Doctor), Dec. 14
Josaphat (Bishop and Martyr), Nov. 12
Joseph (Husband of Mary), Mar. 19
Joseph Calasanz (Priest), Aug. 25
Joseph the Worker, May 1
Juan Diego, Bl. (Layman), Dec. 9
Jude (Apostles), Oct. 28
Justin (Martyr), June 1
Kateri Tekakwitha, Bl. (Virgin), July 14
Katherine Drexel, Bl. (Virgin and Religious), Mar. 3
Lawrence (Deacon and Martyr), Aug. 10
Lawrence of Brindisi (Priest and Doctor), July 21
Leo the Great (Pope and Doctor), Nov. 10
Louis of France (King), Aug. 25
Lucy (Virgin and Martyr), Dec. 13
Luke (Evangelist), Oct. 18
Marcellinus (Priest and Martyr) and Peter (Exorcist and Mar-
    tyr), June 2
Margaret Mary Alacoque (Virgin and Religious), Oct. 16
Margaret of Scotland (Queen), Nov. 16
Maria Goretti (Virgin and Martyr), July 6
Mark (Evangelist), Apr. 25
Martha (Sister of Lazarus and Mary Magdalene), July 29

Martin I (Pope and Martyr), Apr. 13
Martin de Porres (Lay and Religious Brother), Nov. 3
Martin of Tours (Bishop), Nov. 11
Martyrs of Rome, June 30
Mary Magdalene (Witness of the Resurrection), July 22
Mary Magdalene de Pazzi (Virgin and Mystic), May 25
Matthew (Apostle and Evangelist), Sept. 21
Matthias (Apostle), May 14
Maximilian Kolbe (Priest and Martyr), Aug. 14
Methodius (Missionary and Bishop), Feb. 14
Michael, Gabriel, and Raphael (Archangels), Sept. 29
Miguel Pro, Bl. (Priest and Martyr), Nov. 23
Monica (Laywoman), Aug. 27
Nereus and Achilleus (Martyrs), May 12
Nicholas (Bishop), Dec. 6
Norbert (Bishop), June 6
Pancras (Martyr), May 12
Patrick (Missionary and Bishop), Mar. 17
Paul (Apostle and Martyr), June 29
Paul Miki and Companions (Martyrs), Feb. 6
Paul of the Cross (Priest and Founder), Oct. 20
Paulinus of Nola (Bishop), June 22
Perpetua and Felicity (Martyrs), Mar. 7
Peter (Exorcist and Martyr), June 2
Peter Canisius (Priest and Doctor), Dec. 21
Peter Chanel (Priest and Martyr), Apr. 28
Peter Chrysologus (Bishop and Doctor), July 30
Peter Claver (Priest and Missionary), Sept. 9
Peter Damian (Bishop and Doctor), Feb. 21
Peter and Paul (Apostles and Martyrs), June 29
Philip Neri (Priest and Founder), May 26
Philip and James (Apostles), May 3
Pius V (Pope), Apr. 30
Pius X (Pope), Aug. 21
Polycarp (Bishop and Martyr), Feb. 23
Pontian (Pope and Martyr) and Hippolytus (Martyr), Aug. 13

Raymond (Bishop and Religious), Jan. 7
Robert Bellarmine (Bishop and Doctor), Sept. 17
Romuald (Abbot), June 19
Rose of Lima (Virgin), Aug. 23
Rose Philippine Duchesne (Virgin and Religious), Nov. 18
Scholastica (Virgin and Foundress), Feb. 10
Sebastian (Martyr), Jan. 20
Seven Founders of the Order of Servites (Religious), Feb. 17
Simon and Jude (Apostles), Oct. 28
Sixtus and Companions (Martyrs), Aug. 7
Stanislaus (Bishop and Martyr), Apr. 11
Stephen (King), Aug. 16
Stephen (Proto-Martyr), Dec. 26
Sylvester (Pope), Dec. 31
Teresa of Avila (Virgin and Doctor), Oct. 15
Thomas (Apostle and Martyr), July 3
Thomas Aquinas (Priest and Doctor), Jan. 28
Thomas Becket (Bishop and Martyr), Dec. 29
Thomas More (Martyr), June 22
Thérèse of Lisieux (Religious), Oct. 1
Timothy and Titus (Bishops), Jan. 26
Titus (Bishop), Jan. 26
Turibius of Mongrovejo (Bishop), Mar. 23
Vincent (Deacon and Martyr), Jan. 22
Vincent Ferrer (Priest), Apr. 5
Vincent de Paul (Priest and Founder), Sept. 27
Wenceslaus (King and Martyr), Sept. 28

Recommended Reading

Any Friend of God's Is a Friend of Mine, Patrick Madrid (Basilica Press).

By What Authority? An Evangelical Discovers Tradition, Mark Shea (Our Sunday Visitor).

Catholic for a Reason, Leon Suprenant, Scott Hahn, et al. (Emmaus Road).

A Father Who Keeps His Promises, Scott Hahn (Servant).

The Fathers of the Church, Mike Aquilina (Our Sunday Visitor).

Jesus, Peter & the Keys, David Hess, et al., (Queenship).

Mary and the Fathers of the Church, Luigi Gambero (Ignatius Press).

Not by Scripture Alone, Robert Sungenis, Patrick Madrid, et al. (Queenship).

Pope Fiction: Answers to 30 Myths and Misconceptions About the Papacy, Patrick Madrid (Basilica Press).

Rome Sweet Home, Scott & Kimberly Hahn (Ignatius Press).

Springtime of Evangelization, Pope John Paul II, introduced by Thomas Williams, L.C. (Basilica Press).

Surprised by Truth: 11 Converts Give the Biblical and Historical Reasons for Becoming Catholic, Patrick Madrid (Basilica Press).

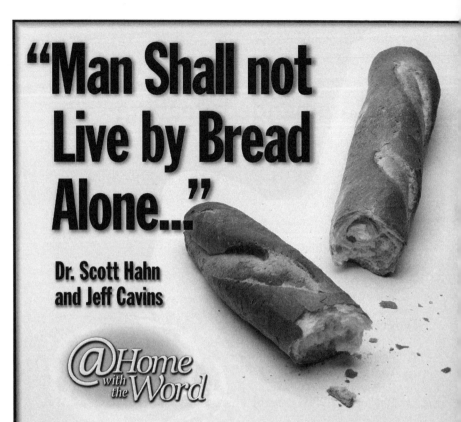

"Man Shall not Live by Bread Alone..."

Dr. Scott Hahn and Jeff Cavins

@Home with the Word

*J*esus spent forty days fasting in the desert, with the Devil tempting Him to turn stones into loaves of bread. Jesus responded, "Man shall not live by bread alone, but by every word that proceeds from the mouth of God" (Matthew 4:4).

Earthly food keeps our bodies running but, like our bodies, it's perishable. Our souls, however, are immortal. They need immortal sustenance: the life-giving Word of God.

The Missionaries of Faith Foundation is excited to bring you the Word of God in a new, powerful weekly Internet Bible study conducted by Dr. Scott Hahn and Jeff Cavins. It's called *@Home with the Word.*

@Home with the Word is ideal for both group and individual study. Each week Scott Hahn and Jeff Cavins present a passage from the Bible, along with its historical background. They provide tips for understanding the meaning of the passage and make important connections to the Catechism of the Catholic Church, papal writings, the Church Fathers, and the Saints. The program also provides discussion questions, which you can explore on your own or as part of a group.

@Home with the Word also provides:

Family Night: This user-friendly weekly program helps families come together to study the Word of God, and discuss important issues facing today's Catholic family. Family activity suggestions also help to bring God's Word home to you and your children.

Parish Partnership: Everyone in your parish can benefit from this program. It features free homily help for priests, a listing of Bible studies in your area, and a question & answer forum called **Truth Tracts.** Your questions about the Bible and the Church are answered by Dr. Hahn, Jeff Cavins, Mark Shea, Patrick Madrid, Matthew Pinto, and other Missionaries of Faith Foundation staff members.

The monthly cost for *@Home with the Word* is just $7.

For more information, call the Missionaries of Faith Foundation at (888) 41-FAITH (888-413-2494) or subscribe at www.moff.org.

Missionaries of Faith
FOUNDATION

Basilica Press books and tapes are available
at your local Catholic bookseller.

To get a free resource catalogue of other Basilica Press
books and tapes, please contact:

Basilica Press
P.O. Box 675205
Rancho Santa Fe, CA 92067

www.basilica.com

Or call us toll-free at

888-396-2339

Do you know someone whose Catholic Faith ended here?

If you're like most Catholics, your answer is "yes" — a family member, friend, or co-worker.

Now you can do something about it. You can bring them home to the Church with *Envoy* magazine, an exciting bi-monthly journal of Catholic apologetics and evangelization.

Edited by Patrick Madrid, internationally-known Catholic speaker and writer, and editor of the best-selling book *Surprised by Truth*, *Envoy* magazine will teach you how to explain and defend Catholic truth in a way that works. Each issue gives you cutting-edge information and answers from today's top Catholic apologists, evangelists, and writers. Our articles are consistently fresh, upbeat, useful, and *charitable*.

Envoy magazine will show you how to explain your Catholic Faith intelligently, defend it charitably, and share it *effectively* — it will prepare you to be an ambassador for Christ.

Subscribe today, and the next time you're faced with friends or loved ones who have lost their Catholic Faith (if not their First Communion picture), you can answer their questions and be a light to guide them home.

To Subscribe Call 1-800-55ENVOY

Bringing Christ to the World